We lo

We love you Michael

James Gibbs

ISBN 1-59109-305-8

We love you Michael

Table of Content

Foreword

Through all the travels and all the troubling times, black music kept me steady. It was the one thing that kept me off the edge in the Nam. Motown artists were a major influence, along with James Brown, Curtis Mayfield, the Ojays, the Impressions, Aretha Franklin, Gladis Knight and too many others to name. Michael has been a constant from my young adulthood right through to now. Other than job training and education, and what one chooses to do as a profession, music is the centerpiece of black culture. During the civil rights struggle, it reached the level of prophecy. I fell in love with R and B at a young age. The last music influence on me was rap. I discovered that it has become the new platform of black urban expression. That and because of my love of rhyme is why I chose it as my medium. I do not think my technique is exact as that used in rap, but there is overflow between the two.

I had seen his Bucharest concert when he performed that fabulous air stunt. I had seen him at the ninety-two presidential inauguration celebrations. I had seen him perform at the Super Bowl. He appeared destined for success no matter what road he took. He was a world class super performer whose very presence generated excitement. Everywhere his feet touched the ground the international press followed. He sipped tea with royalty, shook hands with world leaders; people mobbed him wherever he went. Tens of thousands turned out to see him perform. He was the golden boy with the platinum touch. Was I proud of him – I was. Did I adore him – with all of my heart? Loved all over the world, not just as a performer, but as a humanitarian too, in every country he made headlines. He was the king of his art and he was that by worldwide request. If his work had been less secular it could have earned him sainthood. In person he was shy, but on stage he was explosive.

His achievements go on and on. He seemed unstoppable, but as God had tested Job, he too would be tested, the bomb fell. Like so many of his supporters, I found myself on the defensive. I counterattack blindly without facts. What follows is a lyrical effort to fight that battle. My weapons of choice were rhyme and verse; I attempted to defend and rescue him. The work was a labor in which my passion often pre-empted my judgment, and I admit to prejudice. My walk through his dark times turned into a walk through my own. Did I praise him – I did. Did I criticize him—why not? Did I stay loyal and love him afterward as much – only the pages will tell, but war is hell.

Sometimes because I was angry because of things he did, I tried to compare him to others, and there were many others, all great performers. I had lived through the glory days when the Supremes rocked the nation and the Temptations ruled it with "My Girl." I had seen the wonder boy Stevie Wonder; the Miracles, James Brown and Jackie Wilson; Elvis Presley, the Rolling Stones and the Beatles. All of who left an indelible impression on me, but no one impressed me the way Michael did. So much could be said about his achievements, his family, people in his sphere, and the scandal that drove him into media exile. When his "Thriller Album" set new records in sales, I thought finally talent had overcome race, a talent that was gentle and non-aggressive. I was so entrenched by him that I became more than a fan; I became a worshipper. In that place, in that heaven where I paid him homage, no one came close to unseating him; he was my New World messiah, the good knight. He was touching people all over the world. He was influencing real change, finally breaking down the barriers between entertainment and politics, between music and race. If an old war-horse like Reagen became President because he could manipulate the media, then Michael could have changed the world. That was my hope as I recalled how far we had come since we lost Dr. King. In the arena of entertainment it seemed that the movement hadn't been stalled by murder. Music had produced a black king, the King of Pop. And he did reign but now even that creation was in jeopardy. The fantasy he lived in had become home to so many who wanted to live in a color blinded world. Obviously I was one of those people. What happened to him had a dramatic effect on the stability of my world. Suddenly I felt like I was in a state of war. I prepared myself to do battle. It was on and there was no turning back and so we begin.

This book is dedicated to Michael Jackson whom I have followed for almost 40 years.

No Way Back

Michael has achieved so much and I keep saying that because it's true. So many people love him and I keep saying that because it's true too. In a society like ours where finding outstanding world respected blacks is a difficult task, Michael was one of the few. His awesome talents and his gentle mannerisms made him the choice of both intellectual and average peoples. It wasn't a thing about him being black; everybody knew that fact. To be so looked up to and then for this sudden bad thing to happen, it dropped a dim light on all of blackness. Because he was who he was, people acted like it was to be expected. He was too perfect and this ugly blot made him less so. But I was a true follower and I believed in Michael. No matter what the future brought I would be his confidant. People often made me angry downplaying him to their levels. But true or not true for him the situation spelled out "no way back." The trust he had with children was gone. He had always loved them and shown that through his save the child programs all over the world. All these noble things he had done made it impossible for me to believe he had done this, I couldn't believe it!

> I wasn't going to believe it but a lot of people did
> You're a man Michael—they're not go let you be a kid
> You must from now on keep your great love hid
> I feel like you do and like you I'm thinking God forbid

You Have to Accept the Fact

Undated

I

And he seemed everything
One would expect of a pop king
He was dynamite on stage
Polite, perfect for the new age
In entertainment he was the man
Everybody wanted to be a fan
But then disaster struck
Rode in wit' bad luck
And from a poisoned cup
A great cloud of dirt rose up
It filled the electromagnetic air
Spread like wild fire everywhere
And seeing its brutality
With his downfall almost reality
There was little I could do
But hope it wasn't true
I couldn't help him run
I couldn't undo what had been done
Believing he was the chosen one
I decided to become his poetic gun
Thinking I could influence the vote
Of some future kangaroo court
Everything I heard about him I wrote
I listened to every news report
Often wondering—would there be a trial
He had been accused of molesting a child
A thing by all accounts vile
Some said he was in denial

But he was still my prince
I didn't need to convince
Myself of his innocence
All I could do was go to his defense
So I took on this momentous task
To do for him what he did not ask
What follows is that attempt
Though prejudice I tried to exempt
It warred against my every thought
Believe me I fought
Like so many others I was caught
But I didn't have to be taught
He was the world's greatest performer
The knight who wore no armor
It was a painful melodrama
And I too suffered from its trauma
But having put on my war clothes
Having walked among those
Freedom fighters years ago
I'd thought but now I know
That our fight is not over
We still have to run for cover
We still have to protect each other
On that battlefield he will always be my brother
So I'm raising the colors high
I didn't have time to sigh
The moves I made inside grew
But times were so untrue
It seems every time words fly
We have a new magnetic lie
I asked myself was Dr. King on this earth?
Did I not share that freedom thirst?
Did I not witness civil rights birth?
Can I not see they don't want us first?
If this is where blackness is?
Do I not see the dark abyss?
Do I not recoil from this Judas kiss?

4

Do I not perceive what he can lose in this?
Do I not know what today's racism is?
For no other reason I have a cause in this

II

Being down I felt the hate
It wasn't something I had to debate
Suddenly to be tested by fate
Thousands of miles from where I ate
The strangeness of God I did despair
Yet all men breathe his air
In my heart I had to care
It was a misfortune I had to share
Perhaps on American Bandstand
I saw the future Promised Land
There I became a Michael fan
But that was a distant scan
All I know now is I am
With him a part of the damned
Many years post Vietnam
My weapon is still jammed
I would swim in sewage if it would benefit
Everything the Jacksons made was a hit
I remembered wading through human shit
In a Mai Kong Delta pit
But I never thought I would see him like this
But the tears I saw were his
As I recalled his name on the hit list
The dragon came up out of the mist
It was an evil I didn't want to believe
An evil I didn't want to perceive
But I was too afraid to leave
Too afraid to try to retrieve
The truth that would set us both free
So I too suffered the tyranny
Asking myself how could this be?

It was to him a monstrosity
Michael had been so great
So worshipped here of late
It seems evil couldn't wait
To drag him before its gate
And after great smoke and fury
I found myself on the jury
A part this intense history
But it wasn't a mystery
I believe I understand
We believed we lived in a free land
But not for a black man
Who acts like Peter Pan
And lived in Neverland
In a castle built on West Coast sand
Of whom I am a fan
While his enemies continued raising sand
Most of us were far away
In Europe, the Orient, the USA
As far away as Australia okay
We never thought we would see this day
It looked racist yet to him color was dead
But I fear for what might be ahead
Truly it could be dread
If he were confined fear would spread
And the kingdom could fall
He had to play ball
He had to play to save us all
We awaited the call
To battle knowing we may perish
What he had given us we cherish
I asked does the world know what fear is?
Does it care after seeing his tears?
The media attacked him on the road
With his burden near overload
The shame of it could explode
We spoke to him but did he understand our code?

III

If I had a weapon it would be
Something the eyes could see
Past this how to turn the key
And keep this kingdom free
Free so we may dance
Free so we may glance
The belief that all will have a chance
In this kingdom to advance
Yet while we're smiling
There is racial profiling
Enemies are beguiling
Our forces and styling
Like God gave them a mission
While we stand on tradition
Evil doesn't need permission
It will strike a weak condition
Yet the road before us is straight
We must carry this great weight
Move this awesome freight
We must fight perdition because that's our fate
We the smallest in the kingdom
Insignificant to Swingdom
We can't escape this syndrome
Nor forget where we're from
So we say long live the king
And long may he reign
This is the song we sing
In every battle campaign
For many days we've stood alone
For him we're trying to be strong
We keep on holding on
'Cause he's our last song
Our last chance to overcome
We hear the same drum

The same call to freedom
We have followed him from the slum
Commonality keeps us hanging on
It will carry us back to the throne
Back to freedom's home
Hopefully never again to roam
These dark dungeons of despair
All we need do now is care
Care for him everywhere
All over this world the atmosphere
Calls for his liberation
We must save his music nation
There can be no contemplation
Of defeat if so the annihilation
Planned will destroy us all
Therefore we must stand tall
We must not allow him to fall
We must keep his records in the mall
So they can be accessed
And by doing that we will be blessed
This evil will be dispossessed
His dreams to us will be manifested
But if we lose him I don't know
How much further we can go
How much bigger we will grow
I can't see through God's window
I'm just an average man
To him I'm only a fan
I have no fortunes to command
But as a warrior I understand
That his is a noble sacrifice
For him I will give up the comforts of this life
For what he represents I will pay that price
I will fall on that knife
He's too beautiful to be destroyed
Look at what we have enjoyed
Yes we are annoyed

But we are in a void
We are not paranoid
The will we follow is that of God

Chorus

I know you're suffering from this attack
It doesn't matter about your act
You have to accept the fact that you are black
You're out there with no way back
I know you're suffering from this attack
It doesn't matter about your act
You have to accept the fact that you are black
You're out there with no way back

The End

Make You Feel Less Than A Human Being

Undated

I

How many been close to you
Other than your brothers only a few
People that you knew
People don't know you like they do
You see on a personal level
Only God and the devil
Could be that clever
In this world you may never
Walk undisguised down the street
Or talk to people you meet
You're not an ordinary freak
You're the freak of the week
And though you're not strange
The world won't change
It's too hard to rearrange
Your life will be strange
In ways I can't imagine to see
I don't have extrasensory
Or nothing of such intensity
That would allow me to see
Beyond what I see ordinarily
But I know you're lonely
And most times you only
Want to be what you cannot be
Yes my king I can see
You will never be as free as me
And I'm sorry MJ
Sorry things are that way

But night ain't day
Things develop and decay
There are constants too
And one of them is you
You see no matter where you go
You mean a lot to people you don't know
You're in their daily lives and so
It's the price you pay for your great show

II

I apologize for worshipping you
You're only a man but it's also true
That half the world is watching you
Watching everything you say or do
You live in an amusement park
To a child you are a light in the dark
To the rest of us you're that spark
You're the man we chose as monarch
Chosen because people love you
Chosen because of what you do
I know you have withdrew
You are no longer in my view
But that don't stop us from loving you
And it won't stop us from seeking you
There are false things out there too
But to us you have always been true
I see this darkness coming in
Darker and darker around the bend
This trouble may never end
But if all you wanted was a friend?
I was dedicated to you
And what I feel for you is true
But you got your point of view
You know what you're use to
Those things are never in a fan's view

About your personal life we have no clue
The media speaks for you
And you know how the media do
It can build or destroy you
There's nothing we can do
If it decides to harm you
We can't prove it untrue
We don't get to talk to you
That's what they do
They have that power over you
And that power is what we view

III

You been in show bizness all your life
And you have yet to take a wife
Sure you've been through strife
But what do you know about my life
When your heart breaks mine breaks
It breaks from your mistakes
But do you really feel my aches
Look at these rakes
Piling trash all around
We need a burn down
I will protect the crown
They won't bring you down
Around the kingdom you may never see me
What they show is not who I'm trying to be
I'm in your service secretly
With others like me we guard the key
We know what you're suppose to be
We know how badly
You want to be free
But the kingdom isn't what some see
It's what we feel inside
The greatest thing you've given us is pride

That pride I will not hide
No matter what the courts decide
Sometimes life is like a rubber mat
You have to bounce back
And I'm not shook by that
I will fight for your act
I know jealousy when I see it
They envy if they can't be it
They come up with some phony charge
They make it big and large
When in truth it's just a mirage
Used to steal your George
But this thing you cannot dodge
The enemy has surrounded your lodge

Chorus

My king this is the first time you've seen
That they can make you feel less than a human being
My king some knights are not fleeing
We will stay with you because you are a great being
If you change the locks we will see to the new keying
No one will enter without our seeing
My king this is the first time you've seen
That they can make you feel less than a human being

The End

Accusation and Response

I think Michael was his most attractive when he did "The Thriller" video—not knowing the transformation sequence in the video would one day forecast a similar change in his real life. Michael had a strong desire to feel universal. He didn't want to be controlled or influenced by the racial barriers that the rest of us are subjected to all of our lives. But the thing that almost led to his undoing was not having a chance to grow up in the usual fashion. He lost out on childhood and was determined to regain it back. That's why he had children as friends. He still regardless of the face he had to put on as a professional wanted to be a child. Neverland was the tree house he never had. The amusement park around it was the playground he had to omit. The Bible says when you become a man you have to put away childish things. Michael adapted this axiom late and didn't do so until this tragedy forced it upon him.

Like fans around the world I went through shock. I was forced to do my own analysis and determine for myself the validity of what the media projected as truth. Michael is a pure heart who greatly loves children; I couldn't imagine anything worse that could have happened to him than being seen as some kind of child predator. To be denied the one thing in which he found solace must have been almost unbearable and it probably broke his heart thousands of times. But Michael wasn't in pain alone, we felt his pain; we knew his isolation, and I wanted him to know that we did. In the future hundreds of Michael Jackson websites would pop up all over the world filled and run by people who loved and respected him. But in 1993 that was not evident, the largeness and ugliness of the allegation was something that I had to fight day and night. I sometimes think I would have deserted my own family to save him but thank God I didn't have to and so we continue.

Long Live the King

12/05/93

I

What can I say?
It was Judgment Day
For him in LA
That's the way it was okay
They said he was gay
They wanted him to pay
So they sent their birds of prey
Cameras are that today
They fly overhead
They butter their bread
With every spread
They can raise the dead
They can't be stopped by lead
They're protected by the fed
That's a presidential dread
You are not safe in bed
Their lies will be read
So Michael fled
Like Peter by Hook
His ship was took
His confidence was shook
His treasures stolen by a pirate crook
So the leaves of misfortune fell down
They covered the ground
LA was a poison town
He couldn't rebound
There was trouble all around
He could've lost the crown

So he fled from that trauma
And in this warlike drama
Of pressure and plunder
Drugs almost took him under
That's the power of blunder
It comes with thunder
Ten years was the number
Of the promised coma
Incarceration was a life threatening drama
Yet a friend and his sweet mama
Kept him from going under
So if it were your life what would you do
If you were facing an untrue
Captured by its taboo
And going to court was a booboo
They'd already locked up 32
And they wanted you too in their zoo
Wouldn't it call for voodoo?
Wouldn't it call for juju?
Wouldn't it call for a screw?
What would a smooth criminal do?
Probably call out a wrecking crew
Have them wreck somebody for you
That would've been the end to that
But luckily he is a wealthy cat
I mean he's got major jack
Still he needed someone to watch his back
Something I wanted to do in time
After I dropped this rhyme
The guy was in his prime
And he was crippled by this alleged crime
They didn't care whether it happened or not
They went to the foul line and took the shot
But with the money he's got
Johnny untied the knot
You know what's funny
It was all about money

That's the turnkey
All I have is my poetry
Yet I'm on the battlefield
Using my words as a shield
And I will stay until
The badness is killed
I use words but I'm not a secretary
And perhaps I've drank too much Bloody Mary
What happened was extra ordinary
And though it was contrary
To what my life is about
I have come here to shout
As long as there's a doubt
I won't turn him out
Though this thing interferes
I have been loyal to him for years
I hurt when I saw his tears
And I do have my fears
If this thing every clears
I'll be on the mountain of cheers

II

Consider no one is exempt
From being a wimp
From being a nymph
From being filmed by the Good Year Blimp
Strange—his best friend was a chimp
Reportedly women made him limp
They called him a child pimp
They held him in great contempt
But if you had worked that hard
Got a prestigious music award
Then some big mouth security guard
Said something and your reward
Looked like ten years on a prison yard

Where a pretty boy is a reward
For some convict retard
If you were facing that void
Wouldn't you lose your faith in God?
Molestation is a serious crime
And it carries serious time
You can lose your prime
Just like dropping a dime
And things won't be fine
There are dollars on the line
And for you it's show time
You got to pay the fine
They're not gon' change their mind
That's the eight ball you're behind
You're one of a kind
You can't afford to be blind
The trap was well designed
And if you get off this time
Make sure there's no more monkeyshine
You can't prove you didn't commit a crime
If you go to court you could face prison time
Yo! Listen to my rhyme
It's the shirt off your back
And because you're black
You can't be slack
Not when you're the Mack
Every since they brought us to this place
It's been a slap in the face
Look at what has happened to our race
Africa was once our ace
But we lost that control
In a slave ship hole
Diseased, wet and cold
Then after being on the whipping pole
You do what you're told
I understand why you wanna be bold
But is that worth your soul

They only want your gold
When you're ashy and old
You'll look back and behold
It was what the public was told
And in that you had no control
They treated you cold
Reaped havoc on your soul
But you starred in the Super Bowl
You got the money to pay this toll
You'll have to buy what shouldn't be sold
Still you're connected to Rock
Your fans are in shock
But with every tic tock
That passes off the clock
Our strength grows and will break this lock
I know you're not Mr. Spock
Still some think you can't lie
While others wanna know why
You got prescription high
They didn't see you fall out of the sky
With your head on fire
Entertaining is your greatest desire
But the way things have gone
You landed in a twilight zone
But you need to come home
Together we can stop this syndrome
You can't defeat it alone
You can't defeat it from Rome
Even though you're strong
Your best defense is to come home
Or soon your freedom will be gone
Michael, please come home

III

I hate that the police
After the Rodney King release
Are using you for grease
Will bullshit ever cease?
I dreamed I was in Niece
Someone from the Middle East
Was talking about the beast
I had heard that same talk in Greece
And in this imaginary play
They asked about MJ
They asked if he was okay
But when they mentioned LA
Reality hit and I said okay
They're calling him a pedophile gay
And LA ain't the Bay
No! I don't know if he's gay
That's just what they say
It's okay with me either way
I'm not the one he's got to pay
I'm not some vulture in LA
I'm not working for the DA
I'm not working for the DEA
I'm not working for the CIA
I'm not indebted in anyway
But it's crazy over there okay
So I had to getaway
I'm here on holiday
I couldn't take anymore decay
That's what it was okay
That's what it was in LA
God knows I pray
I feel bad for MJ
I wish they'd leave him alone
But they want his throne

They want his royalty
And his sovereignty
And his fans loyalty
Destroyed—destroying a black is not a novelty
You tell me how he can be
Everybody's cup of tea?
I want him to be free
He is a king to me
And he's gon' be
Respected by me
He's where few blacks get to be
He has world respectability
They're afraid of that—you see
He can influence worldwide reality
So they can't let him be
They want him down on one knee
Begging them to let him be
Hating him because he's free
Because he's living a fantasy
That makes him an enemy
Oh I suppose
Heaven knows
If Michael goes
The kingdom folds
Listen Negroes
Not many of us are pros
That's why I propose
If Michael goes
The fantasy he started
Will soon be departed
Millions will wind up broken hearted
A great love will be discarded
So the loss we face
Will weaken our power base
If he doesn't settle this case
If it ends in disgrace
Then another black we believed in

Will wind up in the pen
Not only will we lose a great friend
A part of Dr King's dream will end

Bridge

So long live the King of Pop—long live the King
So long live the King of Pop—long live the King
And may he keep on doing his thing as long as he is the
king
And may he keep on doing his thing as long as he is the
king

The End

It Was In Bucharest

Undated

I

Heroes don't come everyday
So I'm defending MJ
In the only way
I know how okay
I write about him every day
That's the way I feel okay
So with no more foreplay
Here's what I got to say
He's been subdued
Talked about and treated rude
And I conclude
It's been done with an attitude
But when it's reviewed
You'll see that he was screwed
Why are these cops acting so snood?
Why are they trying to set the mood?
Busting down the door
Running across the floor
Trying their best to score
A criminal encore
To frighten him before
He leaves this candy store
Sail for a distant shore
And live here no more
I'm not saying that all of them are bad
But a lot of them are making me mad
It's a shame how they tore up his pad
Seems they have to make him look bad

II

Now after seeing the Rodney King tape
I knew Michael had to escape
There was almost a congressional debate
Going on around his estate
He wasn't in the best of shape
Across the national landscape
Cameras and press vultures hide in wait
Police were stalking him for the state
But it was in Bucharest
That I saw him at his best
In that rocket-man vest
He was a hero from the west
It was a magnificent quest
His foes had to confess
He was ahead of the rest
He was the absolute best
If a challenge came
It got lost in his fame
He really had game
His whole family has that acclaim
Still in America frame by frame
They showed him in shame
Now when his attackers took aim
With a thirteen year old in their campaign
They started a runaway train
Accusations nearly drove Michael insane
They fell like acid rain
Causing a burning pain
And while he struggled to maintain
They chilled and drank champagne

III

He hated being labeled black
Loved children despite the fact
Of being accused of this monstrous act
But he couldn't counter attack
He had an addiction problem
Things were wrong and he couldn't solve them
His attackers knew the media would mob him
Knowing about his addiction decided to rob him
Using a social worker from the state
To make it look straight
They dropped their anchor weight
When the cops stormed the Neverland Gate
It produced a media swarm
In a state climatically warm
He simply lost his calm
They came like Saddam with Islam
Suddenly everybody with a fairy tale
Had something to sell
They gave him hell
The police wanted him in jail
The tube went elastic
It was so fantastic
They didn't mask it
We didn't ask it
They came with a head basket
A shovel and a casket
If the Simpson case hadn't interfered
The way Michael was being smeared
His case would have never cleared
He was a sheep about to be sheared

Chorus

Before all this mess—he was at his best in Bucharest
Before all this mess—he was at his best in Bucharest
When he left the stage in that rocket man vest
The fans screamed! He was at his best in Bucharest

The End

We Will Pay the Price

11/27/93

I

Early on let me say
Before this thing came his way
We all loved M J
No one talked of him being gay
But that was yesterday
Now today in LA
The city of stars
Limousine cars
All night nudity bars
The city of Star Wars
Yet before Hun Solo
Came to the picture show
Michael had that flow
Michael had that glow
He wasn't broken hearted
His career jumpstarted
After he and J 5 parted
The course he charted
Took him to the stars
Through disco techs and bars
Drums and rock guitars
He became one of the superstars
Now they're trying to exploit
This guy who made it in Detroit
Who has always done for good
But somehow he was misunderstood
I would ask him if I could
With certainty I really would

I would ask him is it true?
Or are they framing you?
The way they're claiming you
Did what I know you could not do
It is making me so blue
Seeing what they're doing to you
But the world hasn't forgot
It cannot and will not
Forget your contributions
Your save the world solutions
Your music and your art
The peace that you impart
Comes from a good heart
You've stayed on the chart
With every hit born
You've given us less to mourn
The costumes you have worn
May be tattered and torn
But by us no less adorn
To you my king we are sworn
And above everything
As long as we have swing
As long as you bring what you bring
You will be our king

II

I feel like a historian
Talking about the story and
The much deserved glory and
Hoping all will understand
Michael to me is no mere man
He comes from Neverland
He is a self made Peter Pan
He wants to make every child his fan
He has given his wealth

To redeem the health
Of children so close to death
So close to their final breath
It really hurts me seeing him torn apart
It's breaking my heart
How can the media discard
One who has worked so hard?
Who played the perfect card?
Received the Lifetime Grammy Achievement Award
You see I have to respect MJ
For where he is today
I can't stop them from playing their little game
I can't stop them from scandalizing his name
But I believe they're on his back
That he's suffering this attack
Mainly because he's black
Since he moved from that Gary shack
Since he set up on that Pacific track
Those jealous and slack
Have been trying to attack
Their purpose is to drive him back
You can be too successful
Just when it's peaceful and restful
Just when you've earned that rest
The way it is in the west
You don't receive the blessed
Instead you're put to the test
Because of their hopelessness
They destroy and divest
In these fever minded herds
Bullets can be words
The condemnation in their verbs
Poisons like poison herbs
So they can kill with their words
Yet as MJ nerds
We hold strong our passion
Whipping blacks is still in fashion

They want you if you play a fool
They're not gon' let Michael rule
They fear him because he's a jewel
And they're cruel
They kill for fuel
They don't want his plan of renewal

III

TV brought pain
The tears came
Like a hard rain
They washed away my refrain
How can he sustain
Himself against this vicious campaign?
He cried but no one came
No one honored his name
I felt his shame
Suddenly he had lost all acclaim
How could one with such fame
Be so easy to frame?
It was an evil game
All focal points the same
Though he prayed long and hard
No answer came from God
Maybe he dressed too mod
He couldn't go forward
They kept calling him odd
A prisoner in his own yard
On my knees I cried out Lord
Give him strength to record
Every note and every chord
Let him use his talent as a sword
And destroy this evil horde
Or let me oh precious Lord
I will break their ranks

I will trample their tanks
I will rob their banks
Take their pounds, dollars and franks
How can I live witnessing this wrong?
How can I listen to this heartbreaking song?
I have tried my best to be strong
But this hell keeps going on and on
I want to rescue my king
I want to fight this evil thing
I want to save the world of swing
I won't let them destroy my king
Yes my God I'm ready to fight
But who is this triple K Knight?
Who claims he's for justice and right
Things good in all men's sight
Yet for the cause of freedom
Michael must overcome
He must defeat this syndrome
He can't stay in Rome
And when he comes home
Lord I ask you to make me strong
I want to help him to carry on
I want to help save his throne
I won't let him face heartache alone
Oh God I beg you, make me strong

Chorus

You of evil recognize
Before blood stains my knife
There's more to life
Than corruption and vice
There is human sacrifice

We are willing to pay the price
We are willing to pay the price
Because Michael is that nice
We are willing to pay the price
All I have I will sacrifice

The End

I'm Here For You Michael

Undated

I

With dirt on his name
Personal hurt came
And in that far out lane
He almost went insane
I'm not Captain Kirk today
I can't beam myself away
From this hurt in LA
I hate them MJ
I don't believe them anyway
No matter what they say
Print in the USA
The USA Today
Isn't suppose to be a dirty rag
But I'm giving it that toe tag
I hear the brag
I hear them saying molestation is your bag
I know what it is
They want to make your money his
The drugs had you in such a state of thoughtless bliss
Before you realized it this thing crept up out of the mist
So now you must protect yourself
And you must do so 'til this darkness has left
You must stay in the light
Who knows what waits up out of sight?
They will hurt you for spite
I know it's not right
That's why I'm here to fight
I'm from the kingdom and I'm a pop-true knight

II

How is this game to be played?
Hearsay is an offer was made
Three hundred grand not paid
Not enough for seventh grade
Who will need counseling they say
Is a million three okay?
Are shrinks that expensive in LA?
Does therapy cost like that today?
From what I know I know MJ
And I know he will pay
To get them to stop calling him gay
For him it's judgment day
He's their government grant
The boy's daddy's a Fire Ant
You know the slant
He used his kid as a plant
I don't see it no-other way
Michael's got it and he's got to pay
That's the way it is in LA
If you got money to give away
And someone's daddy writes a play
And a kid plays his role okay
If the social worker knows
Does she know she's dealing with pros?
Who aren't rich but I suppose
That anticipation grows
Every single day
The media attacks MJ
He can't getaway
When his face reflects like day

III

He didn't have to do the surgery
Do you think a jury
Midst a feeding fury
Won't say we're from Missouri?
Show us—you know the expression
A moment in reflection
Escaping white aggression
Michael's indiscretion
Poor friendship selection
Made him a target for oppression
Not knowing a friend can be a mistake
They're tying him to the stake
How much more can he take
Before he crosses the point of break
The truth is I don't know
I'm not Pinocchio
My nose won't grow
Even if it did what would it show
I'm just a Negro
I can't make them let him go
If they wanna hang a Negro
They hang a Negro
And it's all for show
A parade for that blind ho
But Michael's got that dough
And that's gon' make them let him go
Know what I'm saying Yo!
That mighty cash flow can get you off
Can get OJ back to playing golf

Bridge

I'm here for you Michael—I'm here to stop this anti
Michael cycle
I'm here for you Michael—I'm here to stop this anti
Michael cycle
I'm here for you Michael—I'm here to stop this anti
Michael cycle
I'm here for you Michael—I'm here to stop this anti
Michael cycle

The End

The Fans Are Important To The Man

11/30/93

I

After being plagued by this cop
He's still the King of Pop
Once he gets going he can't stop
Dancing and spinning like a top
He is addicted to the rock
He rocks around the clock
He's got the groove and the move
And he's got nothing to prove
To save his reputation he's got to land it
That doesn't make him a bandit
Even if he is destined to win
Victory over the trouble he's in
It's gon' take a strong wind
To blow him on track again
Excitement was an old and trusted friend
But this kind of smut can do anybody in
And with all they're doing they say
More outrageous things every day
So what if he wants to stay
Out of harms way
That's what he's doing okay
Do you blame MJ?
Do you care when they say he's gay?
Is it okay with you either way?

II

Rock's in his soul night and day

Janet's got Control and that's doing okay
But that don't make you feel a certain way
Especially when your brother's attacked every day
Hurting so badly he left the stage
Left it because of the conflict and rage
The threat of numbers and beige
Made him turn to a new page
He must do for himself the right thing
When the spotlight puts you in the center ring
And you're not a puppet on a string
And your fans are everything
For them—there's nothing you wouldn't do
Believe me I love him too
He done what he had to do
He didn't want to be judged beside an untrue
That night I saw him boohoo
On the television I knew
He needed freedom too
We all do what we have to do
What you do is up to you
I'm glad you have the freedom too
But Michael needs his freedom just like you
He has a right to it just like you do

III

I don't care if you don't care
I'm not your teddy bear
I ain't gon' be with you everywhere
Trust is something we share
Trust me like I do you
That means believing in me too
What else can you do?
What else can I offer you?
All my life I've tried to give
Control the way I live

I don't know what you'll forgive
But I know the way I live
Won't offend any man
I've done the best I can
I have held myself up as high as I can
But realize I'm just a man
A part of God's great resolve
Trying to answer all my thoughts evolve
But I'm going leave this for him to solve
It takes all my resolve
To try to live and treat people right
I have always been a true knight
A defender of truth and light
And I've tried to used good insight

Chorus

His fans are important to the man
That's why I can't understand
Why they are hurting this man
His fans are important to the man
His fans are important to the man
Yes he is a rich black man
And yes I am a big big fan
His fans are important to the man

The End

I Know What You Did

Undated

I

It wasn't okay with me okay
Every night and every day
I hated the way
They abused MJ
I kept saying ain't no way
This kind of thing could happen in LA
They're saying some child went to play
Sometimes half a world away
With someone suspected of being gay
And for awhile thought to be that way
Yet they trusted MJ
Even though LA isn't the Bay
I'm saying no way
Somebody would trust like that in LA
So much that they would let their child play
With someone they thought was gay
They had to have planned it that way
And so they want MJ to pay
To insure their futures okay
He's got the dough so why not pay
Pay or face the DA
He's black so he's got to pay
He's black so he is their prey
He's black, which makes their set up okay
They can play any game they want to play
That's the unwritten law in LA
That's the way it is okay
You know if I was MJ

I would move far away
I would forget the USA
I would do it today
He's not gon' gets justice here okay
Here we may never be free
Unless you got the key
The money to be free
So I'm telling him don't stay in misery
Do what you got to do
Buy up every clue
It doesn't matter who you think you got to prove it to
The only person you've got to save is you
It's all because of the good old boys
And your ability to destroy white noise
You see with your golden voice
You have become the people's choice

II

In this race and class cold war
Half of us don't know who we are
So they threaten to kill a star
They want to ride around in his car
The one—they didn't earn the money for
He carried moonbeams home in a jar
That's what they are shooting for
Trying to give a star a scar
Trying to hide who they are
Saying he went too far
But what I want to know is how long?
Can we be done wrong?
Sing the same old song?
Meanwhile I'm saying Michael be strong
You're known everywhere
The world does care
And it's at least clear

They can't railroad you here
That would cause an international scare
Even though they got a smear
Even though they got us here
I understand your fear
You're afraid in prison you'll be raped
You're not in good physical shape
And unfortunately you can't escape
Everywhere you go you're being taped
So what is your diplomatic status?
That's the only thing that matters
The only thing on which they can't combat us
Otherwise throw a rock and the glass shatters
When a bomb fall the dust rises
Life is full of surprises
Once we worshipped Isis
You're as rich as pharaoh yet you are the nicest
Person whose ancestors were ever sold for spices
Like me some think you're priceless
What's one child in all the sacrifices?
Think of the black children crippled by covert vices
Anyone can see they set you up
And not gon' let you up
Until you hook them up
Until they get money—nothing is gon' get you up
That's a bitter cup
But that's what's up

III

You see in this way
A sucker is born every day
But I'm not you MJ
You got to play it your way
Do what your lawyers say
If that means you got to pay
Then pay them off okay

That might be your only play
The way it is USA
If you're black I say
Don't worry about wrong or right
Right now you're a fallen knight
That means a knight in flight
They're generating old fright
Leading to a lynch mob appetite
I know you see the light
You can't win this fight
Please pay them -- it's all right
Money is all they want anyway
With the media siding with them every day
You don't stand a chance
I hear the music but it's not your dance
Some want you to hang
You might as well had run a kiddy porno ring
You got to pay them if you ever wanna swing
I believe in my heart that that's the right thing
So raise your glass and drink champagne
You don't have to explain
It's a runaway train
And it's driving you insane
Only those in your family close to your heart
Will stand against those trying to tear it apart
Your music will always go on
Because you're so well known
When you're dead and gone
Future rockers will still remember your throne
And how you turned us on
Not some unproved wrong
That someone seeking money says you brought on
Pay them off and move on
Your life doesn't have to end
I will always be your friend
No matter what you're in
Look at how many times you've been in the top ten

IV

One day all the brothers
May say screw the others
We ain't playing no black and white doubles
We're capable of handling our own troubles
And without a gun
We will meet with other brothers of the sun
I will be your poetic gun
Until your future is won
But if you become unreachable
You will be impeachable
Yet your salvation is reachable
And we are teachable
Show us your true soul
Look at your platinum and gold
Everything you've sold
Janet got with Control
But too many little white lies
And dirt digging spies
Can open suspicious eyes
Can make you compromise
Values you should never advertise
I know you're misunderstood
But you're true and good
For cancer children you've been Robinhood
But that won't do you any good
When a judge knocks on wood
You can't beat the media and the DA
Who are already claiming you're gay
They will treat you bad okay
You know what the verdict is gon' say
Then some dentist playwright
In blood 'til midnight
Who is HIV uptight

Will steal the spotlight
A thirteen-year-old will sing
Do for his father a bad thing
Who do you think they're gonna blame
Arrest and put to shame
And still make a claim
On your wealth and fame?
Damn I know its hell
It's legalized blackmail
So what else is for sale?
Everyday we're setup to fail
Setup to go to jail
Mortgaging our folk's homes to pay bail
I know you would really like to raise hell
But raising hell in all possibility will fail

Bridge

You see I know what you did
With yourself and your id
You went inside yourself and you hid
You crippled your ego amid
The personal crisis into which you slid
The pressure piled on about the kid
Then with drugs you closed the lid
You see I know what you did

The End

Let Me See A Show Of Hands

Undated

I

Johnson and Dempsey
Jackson and Winfrey
Events that took place
That shaped our race
Back to outer space
And lovely Janet's face
I would have never thought
After he fought
After the moonwalk
And all the crazy talk
That they would work together
But the Jacksons are forever
They are first and foremost a family
And that's no fantasy
If Michael never gets amnesty
At least he has a great family
That wouldn't desert him
Except one who wants to hurt him
Whose always been down trodden
A little spoil and little rotten
Gone but not forgotten
She goes around hop scotching
Like a kid playing jumping jacks
She's one of those blacks
That will attack
Anybody to get on track
Family members generally love each other
But in this case—having a famous brother

One that's obviously in trouble
Like any witch she adds a bubble
When you fall back on your family for cover
The one thing you may discover
Is that a sister is not a mother
Especially one with a money hungry lover

II

So how black can this be
If you go back you will see
That black negativity
Is part of the pre-Michael reality
Perhaps we will never be free
Still I search for the key
That will unlock this controversy
They have shown him no mercy
So we have a full-fledged attack
Against another prominent black
The one whose life is on a soundtrack
Though they don't make it look black
On the eighties' time trek
Long before the war with Iraq
The CIA's Contra act
Was built on a cocaine contract
And on us it's had a drastic impact
It broke God's contact
They say the President then didn't know
Didn't know his GI Joe
Fighting south of Mexico
Was paid for by ghetto coke flow
And they're countering on that
Never becoming a stat
Or an acceptable fact
And we all know that
That's where blacks are at

We also know being black
Often draws a negative impact
Upon the social contract
That must be intact
It's not enough to react
You must slam racism to the mat
Every time they attack

III

Suddenly Michael was a mountain
An overflowing fountain
I don't know if he made a mistake
But they didn't give him a break
They tied him to the stake
Tarred and feathered him with debate
Over what for heaven sake
Something on which to speculate
While the oil flowed in Kuwait
The big boys got their piece of cake
Time flows one-way and then the other
So down goes another brother
A Star Spangle Banner lover
Who through pain came to discover
A rose has thorns as well as beauty
And though you're sworn to duty
You go out every day
Prune and cut a way
All which may show up as decay
Still you might not get that perfect bouquet
Such perfection only lasts a day
Because short of Heaven nothing is that way
You think you have friends devoid of your wealth
But your friends are in stealth
And that scares you to death
In fact it's ruining your health

Nothing much was ever said about Elvis's addiction
Heaven protects some angels of affliction
But some must suffer without benediction
Live a long time under the cruelty of fiction
And so it is so in the world of today
That heaven and hell may pass away
But if you are accused of being gay
For you there is a second judgment day

Bridge

To those who would be offended
I'm sorry no harm is intended
But when Michael's case transcended
Retaliation couldn't be suspended
If you won't give into hostile demands
Let me see a show of hands
Stand up if you are his fans
Let me see a show of hands

The End

Answer the Question!

I think anyone personally committed to Michael had to ask the question. We wanted to know was it true? It was a painful time for fans. We saw him on TV, and we wanted to believe, but still what face value could we place on those emotions. At the time we didn't know about his drug problem. All we knew was that he had gotten caught in a compromising position. He was vulnerable but the law must've found nothing in the case to bring to trial. They couldn't find one collaborator. Knowing how sensitive and how private he is, the ordeal must have been overwhelming. Yet as afraid as I was, I wanted to know what the police interrogation felt like. I tried to abandon it but writing 'Answer the Question' was the closest I could imagine to what the police did. To me this particular piece was harmful, but what the police did was harmful, they caused Michael a lot of pain and seeing him caused me a lot of pain, so I decided to include it.

I would like to point out again that this poem though it is harsh represents the kind of things that go on in police station doing an interrogation. I too still recoil every time I read it and I know Michael personally will not like it but I felt it was necessary to examine the full spectrum of events that he was subjected to doing the scandal. Michael is uniquely brave and this poem in a way acknowledges that. Think of yourself going through this kind of treatment if you were innocent. If you were a person held in high regard in almost every country in the world and upon coming home you had to endure this, how would you feel, what would you think?

Answer The Question!

11/27/93

I

Answer the question!
Answer the question!
Why did you buy those toys?
Do you like young boys?
Do you like girls—what's your choice?
Is what you're saying a bunch of noise?
Answer the question!
Answer the question!
Can you name the women
With whom you've been?
Did you enjoy them then
And if you did when?
Answer the question!
Answer the question!
Why couldn't you cope
Without prescription dope?
Do you still have hope
Of being a rock star pope?
Answer the question!
Answer the question!
Why did you cancel your tour?
Do you know and are you sure
Rock and roll can cure
Or is that just a lot of fan manure?
Answer the question!
Answer the question!
What's your thing with Liz?
Do you pay her for the biz?

What did you do at Walt Diz?
Who did you play in the Wiz?
Answer the question!
Answer the question!
Why did you change your face?
Are you ashamed of your race?
Do you hate their social place?
Can you cope with disgrace?
Answer the question!
Answer the question!
Isn't what you're saying baloney?
Aren't you really a phony?
Would you like to call your attorney?
What do you do when you're lonely?
Answer the question!
Answer the question!
Do you think you're white?
Isn't your skin too light?
Do you sleep at night?
Why is your mind in flight?
Answer the question!
Answer the question!

II

Answer the question!
Answer the question!
Are you a pimp?
Why did you have a chimp?
Was he tax exempt?
Do you feel any contempt?
Answer the question!
Answer the question!
Do you love any ho?
Did you love Bo?
And did you know

You're still a Negro!
Answer the question!
Answer the question!
How much money have you got?
Is ten millions a lot?
Why did Pepsi not
Continue your spot?
Answer the question!
Answer the question!
Did you buy Neverland
So you could play Peter Pan?
Why did you offer that man
Three hundred grand?
Answer the question!
Answer the question!
Did your father abuse you?
Is what your sister said true?
Do your brothers love you
Or are they using you too?
Answer the question!
Answer the question!
How did father treat your mother?
Did he cheat on her?
Have you ever had an adult lover
Or is that just a blur?
Answer the question!
Answer the question!
Have you ever had other affairs
What's in the secret room upstairs?
Do children love you everywhere
Like they love you here?
Answer the question!
Answer the question!
Is there a woman who will testify
That you are a normal guy
Or would that too be a lie
A bought and paid for alibi?

Answer the question!
Answer the question!

III

Answer the question!
Answer the question!
Is what you say in your music true?
Are you true to the red, white and blue?
Why don't you counter sue
Or is that too voodoo for you?
Answer the question!
Answer the question!
Now isn't it a fact
That you haven't been intact?
And did signing that contract
Give Sony control of your act?
Answer the question!
Answer the question!
When you signed with Sony
Was it strictly for the money?
Are most of your days sunny
Or they like gambling money?
Answer the question!
Answer the question!
When you were alone
Did you call this kid on the phone?
Has calling ever been a turn on?
Do you feel phone sex is wrong?
Answer the question!
Answer the question!
Why do you like little boys?
Why do you buy them toys?
Why didn't you change your voice?
Do you support freedom of choice?
Answer the question!

Answer the question!
Do you feel like a child?
Do you get buck wild?
Are you a rich pedophile?
Why do so many like your style?
Answer the question!
Answer the question!
Have you thought about suicide?
Do you have that much pride?
Why do you have to hide?
Do you think we will let you slide?
Answer the question!
Answer the question!
Will you continue to sing?
Do you think you're a king?
Should blacks swing?
Have you ever done the wrong thing?
Answer the question!
Answer the question!

IV

Answer the question!
Answer the question!
What's behind that secret door?
Can you dance on any floor?
Do you always keep score?
Have you paid others off before?
Answer the question!
Answer the question!
Let's talk about this kid
Did you do what they say you did?
And what about your id
Can you keep your true feelings hid?
Answer the question!
Answer the question!

What do you think when a black calls you brother
Do you love your mother?
Should blacks trust each other?
Have you ever had a heterosexual lover?
Answer the question!
Answer the question!
Are you afraid to go to court?
If you go to trial can you get a fair vote?
Have you ever written a suicide note?
How much of your earnings do you report?
Answer the question!
Answer the question!
Do you support the NCF?
What do you think of yourself?
What's on the back shelf?
Is any of your career left?
Answer the question!
Answer the question!
Do you sleep in the dark?
Why did you build that park?
Are you a child shark?
Is the park your Noah's Ark?
Answer the question!
Answer the question!
Do you own any stock?
How do you feel about rock?
Are your fans in shock?
Where is the key to the lock?
Answer the question!
Answer the question!
Who removed your mole?
Did you pay them in gold?
Why aren't your friends old?
Are you warm inside or cold?
Answer the question!
Answer the question!

Chorus

You have the right to remain silent
You have the right to remain silent
You have the right to remain silent and non-violent
You have the right to remain silent
You have the right to remain silent
You have the right to remain silent and non-violent
Answer the question Mister answer the question!
Answer the question Mister answer the question!

The End

It Was Like Lights, Cameras, Action

Undated

I

They were amazed that intimidation
Brought them no useful information
This increased their frustration
He had survived their interrogation
He withstood the questioning alone
He had been in their twilight zone
Near exhaustion he went home
They got nothing but the syndrome
They went on and bugged his phone
Michael suffered these abuses alone
You know they were wrong
Luckily Michael was strong
They got nothing to go on
And having found nothing wrong
They couldn't rival the throne
They had to leave him alone
And the Press was there for that
He was a rich and famous cat
They had treated him like a rat
Nevertheless they had to scat
Attorneys discussed it over the phone
What he settled for is unknown
All we know is some money is gone
It changed hands and life goes on

II

Michael hadn't been caught
The lesson had been taught
No matter what they thought
They don't know what he bought
Money can do that see
Strong currency can break you off free
To the cops you're history
Another unsolved mystery
For years he went undercover
Nobody knew where he was not even his mother
And the Press did bug her
All we knew was he's no longer a drugger
He went to a clinic and got rid of it
He got rid of every bit of it
I'm drug free could be his biggest hit
But we knew he could do it
Sometimes it hurts deep inside
And I really hurt when he cried
They want us to believe he lied
They wanted to make him go someplace and hide
The first time he didn't come was because of dope
This time they almost destroyed his hope
We have no idea of what it takes to cope
Being normal we will never experience that scope

III

My God, My God oh-oh-oh-oh lordy
Not only did they accuse him of being knotty
They photographed his entire body
Now tell me what you think about that Shorty?
They treated him like a piece of meat

How would you've handled that kind of heat?
Having been treated like a freak could you compete?
Michael is kind, gentle and sweet
All he really knows is the beat
He probably never thought about something this deep
They made him feel like a creep
Weak and bare like a furless sheep
He was in there naked and alone
I guess that must've turned them on
You know those cops were wrong
You don't have to ask me I know he's strong
It must have felt like being raped
Everything he said they taped
I don't know if I could've escaped
Michael whole life was re-shaped
I've worked in prisons and I've seen that kind of hate
And for it to happen to somebody that great
What they did seemed racist so I can relate
Being black here is something no black has to debate

Chorus

It was like lights, cameras, action
Hold your arms up Jackson
It was like lights, cameras, action
Hold your legs up Jackson
It was like lights, cameras, action
Hold your penis up Jackson
It was like lights, cameras, action
Bend over and spread 'em Jackson
It was like lights, cameras, action
It was done with a brutal passion

The End

His Daddy Used Drugs On His Son

Undated

I

Before I say I don't know
It happened years ago
They decided to score
He had never faced that before
He was taking a shower
Stayed in about a half an hour
Reached out and grabbed a towel
Like Adam Clayton Powell
Eyes were glued on him
And so little Jungle Jim
Father knew chances were slim
The Press wouldn't believe him
He had spent nights with the superstar
Who would be accused of going too far
The police would mention a penis scar
And like a player knows his guitar
They know where the chords are
Until this no one had gotten that far
No one had threatened the star
He could almost drive freely his car
Without wearing a fat suit
But this little recruit
After his daddy had given him drugs in a shoot
Shot the tap root
Dangling freely in this air
The king was very fair
No marks or moles anywhere
Not even in his hair

Unless you go to the scalp
What about the kid's rap
It was all for the ginger snap
Mostly it was just crap
Put together by his pap
To bridge a monetary gap
The kid might have set on his lap
Looking at comic books where Michael took his nap

II

You know how they do man
That was Neverland
Fighting extortion was never a plan
Michael thought he was a free man
Except when he was with the band
Touring in some other land
He never thought a fan
Would take him down the cop scan
Do you understand?
He's a famous man
Who people loved in every land
On that he thought he could stand
He didn't think about being Afro-American
People love him in Japan
People loved him in Iran
People loved him in Pakistan
People loved him in the Outback land
I mean the man was the man
There was no place on the earth he didn't have a fan
Then they came and talked about putting him in the can
Filmed his penis you understand
When all he did was lead a band
It broke his heart you understand
He has feelings just like we do
He loves America just like we do

What was the man to do?
You know it was a screw
What would you do if someone told you
To undress like you were on Paid for View?
You can see how they tried to step
On him — they knew he had a rep
They knew he wanted his personal life kept
Johnny came and he got some help
Johnny was a man who never slept
He seemed to make the opposition feel inept

III

Yes I wonder what the boy saw
Do you think it was something raw?
Does being naked break the law?
Had they found Samson's jackass jaw?
Something they could kill thousands of fans with
And since was a myth
He should've took the Fifth
But he didn't want to deal with the filth
I know the cops wanted to drop the lid
Tell me do you know the kid?
How long can his daddy keep him hid?
Does the kid know what he did?
I mean the whole world is upset
This was career roulette
Michael's career was the bet
If he's lost he could've never paid the debt
Going back before ninety-six
The boy's father put the devil back in the mix
He was looking for another quick easy fix
He was running the same old six sixty six
You see the man — the playwright
He couldn't sleep at night
He was after more money right

Money gives you that appetite
The first extortion plan they set in motion
Had taken a great portion
Of Michael's money and the notion
Of his lifelong devotion
To children had already come under suspicious eyes
It was all a bunch of lies
The people Michael could have called upon he didn't realize
We would have supported him no matter what the enterprise

Chorus

His daddy used drugs on his son
The kind of fan I am I would've thought of a gun
But thank God I wasn't there for that LA run
Because I would've protected the one glove one
His daddy used drugs on his son
He didn't use the drugs for fun
He used truth serum on him to get the job done
The child was induced to lie about Mr. Jackson

The End

These Crooks Came Along And Took Him To The Party

Undated

I

Wait a minute June
Shoot me a moon
That was the cartoon
I saw before noon
You see the boy's mother loved Michael too
His daddy was a crook through and through
And a sorry ass dentist too
I've read the dental review
And I'm a dentist too
What could Michael do?
When his attorneys resigned he was through
If a bird shits on you driving down the avenue
There's not a damn thing you can do
Crooks are going to make money off of you
Once they get the right venue
And find you're on the menu
It was a wild situation out west
With the madness that was in the Press
If they conspired against you it's no contest
When prison can become your next address
You try to walk away from the mess
You start a new manifest
And you control how you invest
And you keep a witness
There won't be another attempted arrest
But you got to control your interest
Crooks are out there and I confess

They can make you wear a bulletproof vest
You see what I'm saying June
Back then it was high noon
And you shot Michael a moon
The follow up was to call him a goon

II

Now if Johnny Cockran
Early in the plan
Had met Mr. Rothman
I wouldn't be doing this understand
But when things get built up so high
In the world you think wanna die
Rather than fight your way out of a lie
And you got no alibi
The police keep coming through
And you know they're after you
Your window becomes your only view
Because all the world's watching you
You're treated like a famous outlaw
It's the picture of you that they draw
And the situation has become very raw
Under those circumstances I say F the law
Michael was doing his business overseas
Suddenly in LA there was this disease
Wasn't long before he was in a squeeze
He could even land in the Florida Keyes
Do you understand me Breeze?
The world can be a deep freeze
Everything you got they can seize
You'll be on the spot and on your knees
When they dropped the bomb it blew up all over town
Like an earthquake it could be felt for miles around
It shook the damn ground
And no one knew how things would finally go down

Michael was on his world tour
While around his place, in his face, piled up the manure
Even though the man is pure
Money turned out to be the only cure

III

Let me tell you about this bummer
You write your own number
The boy's stepfather and his mama
Got caught in this get rich drama
At first they didn't believe a word
From his daddy that they heard
But after they found they'd divide a third
Away went that little I won't tell a lie bird
All I can say is that I am
Not surprised by this goddamn scam
Once you get your ass in a jam
It's not like taking a piss exam
With a contaminated cup
They don't tell you what's up
And nobody else gives a fuck
They'll haul your money away in a truck
A man who didn't care about his child
Suddenly developed that caring style
And nobody thought that was wild
They didn't read his crooked smile
Like they might've been chasing a pussycat
They let him set Michael up like that
And Michael flying around as blind as a bat
Didn't know he would be called a flying rat
It happened all because his van
Broke down outside of Neverland
That's the day he met the son of E-van
And the set up was soon in hand
His daddy found the crookedest lawyer he could find

He was not gon' change his mind
You see in the end the bottom line
Is not who you are but whether you can pay the fine?

Chorus

Michael got setup—poor Michael loved everybody
These crooks came along and took him to the party
Michael got setup—poor Michael loved everybody
These crooks came along and took him to the party
Before he knew it they all got shoddy
And just like that they all got snotty
Michael got setup—poor Michael loved everybody
These crooks came along and took him to the party

The End

They Were Breaking Him Down And Making Him Crawl

Undated

I

You understand before he moved in near Hollywood
Michael had no childhood
His daddy made them practice until they were good
As a child he never stood
At the gates of Disneyland
So why is it hard to understand?
That when he became a man
First thing he wanted to do was go to Disneyland
His childhood was arrested
But that was not protested
It was all about what Joe invested
And what Joe manifested
Was work-work-work—work every day
His kids never got away
Not one single day like kids and play
So what more do I need to say
What Joe did was wrong okay
His kids grew up in hotels all across the USA
Joe went out there to get that pay
To do that he made them practice everyday
So Michael's a rich man whose hurt is deep
His climb to success was steep
They practiced before they went to sleep
I have to say Joe was a creep
But that's why Michael's so good on his feet
He was raised strictly by the beat
But as a man he was incomplete

His ties to children was to resolve that delete
He just wanted to be a child
Is that so impossibly wild?
He had enough money for any lifestyle
But the one he chose was to be a child
At least to be one for a little while
Cash money can get you any profile
Cash money can get you any style
Including an amusement park for a child

II

What do you expect when a man goes up under a curse?
Wanting to be a child—a lot of us do a lot worse
He couldn't go see the school's nurse
While others played he had to rehearse
I can't blame Joe for wanting them to be first
I can't blame him for wanting to see that starburst
He had this thing and a very crazy thirst
But none of his boys took that early ride in the hearse
So Michael is different from me
And you too don't you see
His suffering has made him a key
To unlock an understanding that most will never see
He has overcome so much
And he has the sweetest touch
While those who hate him in anger search
On the other side his mama believed in the church
And Michael is more like his mother
He's a quiet very deep lover
Of things most us will never discover
That makes him a very unique brother
Remember Jesus loved children too
So when they gather around you
You can do what Michael would do
Grab them and hold them close to you

I don't really blame this child
Because his daddy went wild
Hooked up with a man with a crooked smile
Extorted Michael to change their lifestyle
But the country had to be sick too
For them to do what they did do
Michael I hate they hurt you
You ended a friendship that comforted you
All because of human greed
And the desire to get things most never need
They came close to destroying a great lead
Michael most of all I want you to succeed

III

Now y'all know y'all know although
Sixty eight grand is a lot of dough
But you wonder if business was slow
Was this man a father or a ho?
How do you get that far behind?
With just six thousand to pay a year at a time
You wonder what was the bottom line.
Why wasn't he charged with a crime?
He never paid his child support, not one-year
It took eight to get him there
He created this Michael scare
It's obvious he didn't care
He used his child to get close to Michael didn't he?
So he could hit him in the kidney
After which he gained a kind of litany
So Michael took the boy to Walt Disney
And he took him to Toys 'R Us
Their relationship was robust
You may say it was to get the boy's trust
And if that's your statement you can feel my disgust
Michael could've taken any child they all love him

This family he got close to them
And the boy really liked him
But his daddy made him another Jungle Jim
To rob the natives I can't forget it
He hit Michael wit' it
Told a tale saying he did it
And God didn't forbid it
His daddy saw a chance to hit it big
So naturally he acted like a pig
Michael was on worldwide gig
Meanwhile the cops started to dig

Chorus

I guess he didn't believe it was happening that's all
He could fight but he had never had to brawl
Every since he could remember he stood tall
They were breaking him down and making him crawl
I guess he didn't believe it was happening that's all
He could fight but he had never had to brawl
Every since he could remember he stood tall
They were breaking him down and making him crawl

The End

His Money Was Already Spent

Undated

I

Look I'm talking about the syndrome
Why don't you get off that phone?
The man tried to get Michael to buy him a home
Told Michael he shouldn't be staying alone
You say Michael was intelligent he knew better
If he believed something that stupid whatever
You say Michael should have gotten it together
But Michael trusted these people—he never
Thought he'd wind up the victim of a devilish plot
All over the world Michael was hot
Why didn't he expect a cheap shot?
I guess in honesty he really forgot
That he was the monarch of a musical Camelot
He wanted to be normal but he was very hot
He couldn't go around a lot
He was trapped and on the spot
You know the drug problem he had
Had really gotten really bad
Especially after the cops raided his pad
He was filled up and he was mad
Here's a man who had excelled in many cultures
The news people were stalking him like hungry vultures
In some places he had sculptures
But in Santa Barbara all he found were these ruptures
Who could he trust after all of this?
They wanted his money but the money was his
He kept asking his mama how they could do this.
She cried with him but the fears were his

The police were doing everything they could
To stop this megastar and children Robinhood
They didn't care about all the good
He had done—they only knew where they stood

II

I wanna say Michael is not a crook
He only paid to keep enemies from getting a closer look
His mama raised him by the good book
Dealing with the lawyers of a ruthless Captain Hook
With his lawyers telling him to pay
Insisting that was the only way he could walk away
Telling him that he didn't have live near LA
And that the police were still trying to get OJ
Sometimes that's the best you can git
If you get caught up in some shit
Near the end most of his lawyers split
What can you do then but deal wit' it
He didn't want to pay—he wanted to fight
But the destruction to his image would've been out of
    sight
Not good for a man of tremendous might
Not good for man hailed higher than any knight
Not even Charles could've faced this one down
Without risking jeopardizing the crown
Michael from a rehab out of town
Saw his whole world tumbling down
Things he had worked years to build
Stood before this beast waiting to be killed
He could find no theme for victory on that field
It was not a campaign in which he was skilled
The boy's daddy had closed his trap
Between truth and fiction there was no gap
Once he drugged the boy and got that crap
All he had to do was spin his rap

Michael was gon' go down
They knew that all over town
We worried that he could lose the crown
Wind up being painted as a deviant clown

III

While Michael had a reputation for lifting people
Rothman, Chandler's attorney had one for stiffing people
He was always slipping people
Most of the times ripping people
On face value he was not a nice guy
People who knew him said he would lie
They also said you couldn't deny
If he wore a white sheet he wore no tie
For something as sensitive as child molestation
Would you trust him in deliberation?
Would you even think to give him the slightest
    consideration?
Unless the two of you cooked up the allegation
While the custody battle went on for the boy
They went on their mission to extort or destroy
To either rob Michael or take away his joy
They knew he loved children and that love would become
    their decoy
When you're rich and isolated and few things give you
    pleasure
And if a child's laughter is something you treasure
Then that love is a feeling that has no measure
There's no value you can put on it except to hold it as a
    treasure
It is a precious and hopefully lasting possession
As smart as people are in love they follow their own
    direction
Often they don't think they need protection
All they think they need is truth and confession

Michael simply thought he could have a second childhood
After all he was traveling the world doing all this good
I didn't say he was perfect and no one should
I just said he traveled the world and did a lot of good
But America is not a place that a black can be a standout
To have great wealth and not be asking for a handout
Michael was living in this dreamland and he never thought
to doubt
That his kindness and generosity could one day turn that
world out

Chorus

Michael's cash was so inviting these white boys started
fighting
That's what I'm writing and that's what I'm reciting
Michael's cash was so inviting these white boys started
fighting
That's what I'm writing and that's what I'm reciting
Considering how much time he spent overseas for drug
abuse treatment
When he came back his money was already spent
It hadn't been spelled out in fine print but that was no
longer the argument
Even though Michael was innocent his money was already
spent

The End

My Main Man

02/02/94

I

You talk about his money
When you should be calling Ronnie
He's your Bugs Bunny
Your cartoon funny
The man who did it for you
But Michael is not through
What they're saying is not true
The kid is a young actor on review
And if he was drugged I'm asking you
Wouldn't you be stereotyped too?
You wanna know the truth
His daddy can fix your tooth
But fourteen ain't uncouth
For an organized youth
Executing a father's plan
To become a rich man
You do Peter Pan
And like the Shah of Iran
If he loses control
The ticket is sold
In the days of old
We had to escape 3 K patrol
If you've lived you paid rent
You didn't pass judgment
But now how can you trust a government
That slam dumps its President
And you can't get the media pissed off
And you can't tell them to kiss off

You have to be your own boss
In these times or you're lost
Understand the situation
When they leaked information
It was character assassination
They couldn't take the humiliation
They had to take after Rodney King
So they went after Swing
Thinking he would be an easy thing
They monitored every phone ring
Hoping to get a break
Water in a dry lake
They created heartache
For him but he did not break
So the cookie didn't crumble
They threatened him with a legal rumble
They wanted him to stumble
But all they heard was his safe tumble

II

Tell me what expense
Is too immense
For a crowned prince
He jumped the fence
He didn't try to convince
A white jury of his innocence
I say without pretense
Use your common sense
He did the right thing
I don't care he's the king
The way he swing
The way he sing
The way he reacted to the syndrome
He used wealth to save the kingdom
You ask what kingdom

The Kingdom of Swingdom
It's yours and mine
It's the rhythm and rhyme
It's how we define
Our relationship to time
The investigation
Of one accusation
No collaboration
Didn't destroy our nation
Didn't stop his reign
Such a thing is insane
Can you explain
Why they are so lame
And so afraid
And so under paid
That they raid
Criminals for aid
I'm not worried
I'm not hurried
The time will come
We all will have freedom
But until that time
It's worth every dime
To stand in line
To see him one more time
He is the king
The king of pop and swing
I want to see him do his thing
I want to hear him sing
And I thank the gods
That he has worked hard
Overcame all the odds
His success is our reward

III

He's the skip
Captain of this ship
Captain on this trip
I said let it rip
Isn't he worth it all?
They made the call
They shot the ball
It bounced off the wall
The money is his
And money has ended this
That's how it is
And like it is
Yes I'm satirical
I have to be lyrical
I'm hysterical
It's a miracle
To get him off
So screw the cost
If he had lost
That would've been the rip off
That would've hurt every fan
He is more than
The simple leader of a band
He's our main man
And I support him
They couldn't out vote him
So they're tried to cut throat him
They want to scapegoat him
But he's still Number One
He's still the top gun
A formal Motown son
Still having fun
As he entertains
And he remains

A positive attribute to black gains
He has championed many campaigns
And he is the top draw
And though they made it raw
Life is a seesaw
So screw John Law
This wasn't about the truth
It wasn't about the youth
They don't want a truce
They want to seduce
The public and destroy him with the abuse
They want him but he keeps busting loose

Bridge

Here's to my man—my main man—my main man
Here's to my man—my main man—my main man
And it's nice to have a man—They can't trash can
Here's to my man—my main man—my main man
Here's to my man—my main man—my main man
And it's nice to have a man—They can't trash can

The End

Support the King

Michael's crisis was my crisis. For me it became a personal attack. I didn't sleep at night. I spent every waking moment worried about the outcome. Was it because he was black and being black I felt what he felt at least in term of having a collective fear. How far could and would I take being a fan. All I could think of was how unfair they were to him. The media seemed bent on destroying him, and with each media attack I became more intense. Every day I rushed home to get the news. Every night, night after night sometimes all night, I watched CNN hoping something would make this ugly thing go away but nothing did. I prepared for war.

What would I do if I couldn't see him anymore? I couldn't say but the thought was too horrible to imagine. I searched my own conscience for answers—they were not there. For certain they had him all they had to do was close the trap and a great part of my life would be lost. I still had his albums but if they were successful there would be no more and what I had would be the last I would get for life. With him in prison the price of even his old works would escalate far beyond my ability to pay. A lot of my records were plastic and the world was progressing toward CD. How long could I listen before my turntable went bad or an album scratched? My depression grew and I couldn't resolve my fear. We could lose him and that lost could be forever.

Let Me Tell You One Thing

01/07/94

I

Shouldn't we be guarding the king?
Let me tell you one thing
Everybody should be guarding the king
The king of pop and swing
Without exception he is very nice
He is being made to pay a heavy price
They sailed on good advice
They were looking for spice
They brought here soul on ice
We were ripped from paradise
Let me tell you one thing
Everybody should be guarding the king
You have seen him swing
You have heard him sing
Let me tell you one thing
Everybody should be guarding the king
Let me tell you one thing
Everybody should be guarding the king
He's the king of pop and swing
And that's not just a black thing

II

After four hundred years
Of blood, sweat and tears
He had risen above fears
To the sound of many cheers
Every time he took the stage

We are lifted into a new age
And placed upon that page
Written by him we can engage
And when he has performed
The world is transformed
The human heart is warmed
And hatred is again disarmed
He is the tutee fruity
The shake your booty
We owe him more than duty
He is a thing of beauty
Confused perhaps aren't we all
After all wasn't Paul
Confused when he was Saul
We must not let him fall

III

Too easily people abort
Time which is already short
Look at what we're being taught
Can we let him be caught
By the injustice of an evil system?
Can we stand by and let him become a victim
No we must change the system
We can't let him be its victim
As long as I can declare I am free
He can depend on me
With few reservations I commit my loyalty
And though his kingdom is not this reality
I confirm his sovereignty
And his leadership in R and B
Truly he is a great soul
From the time his sister released Control
I like the knights of old
Have dedicated myself to this goal

And I will be bold
I will not let them fit me into a mold

IV

Will we let them determine for us
Who is worthy of us?
Do you think we can place our trust
In people who kept us
In the back of the bus?
I feel deeper and deeper disgust
And I'm standing by that
I realize where we are at
Every time one of us comes to bat
The next thing you know you smell a rat
Our leaders have paid an awful price
How many times will they pay it twice?
Always being sort by the Vice
That's the price of soul on ice
But if we stop being down
Stop being for them a clown
We could score the home run
And with others of the sun
Life here too could be fun
If we stop fearing the overseer's gun

Bridge

Let me tell you one thing—Everybody should be guarding
the king
Let me tell you one thing—Everybody should be guarding
the king
Let me tell you one thing—Everybody should be guarding
the king

I'm saying to every single swinging jock that ever felt the
need to rock
Let me tell you one thing—Everybody should be guarding
the king
Just like the hands that sweep the clock we must not stop
supporting rock

The End

You Got To Funk for the Right to Funk

01/29/94

I

There was no let up
In the setup
From the get up
No indictment
No enlight'ment
Just excitement
You say you seek justice
But you pay off
For the lay off
Just to stay off
So quick came the advance
You had no chance
You had to dance
They had the Juice
You couldn't break loose
You are not Muse
Don't risk the goof
They need no proof
It's through the hoof
So funk justice!
Isn't this another attack?
Another knife in the back
Of a prominent black
That they're calling gay?
And he will pay
Or find himself their prey
So funk justice!
The average black

Lives in a shack
Is still held back
But if you make it to the top
Become the King of Pop
And still have to fear the cop?
And can't make them stop
Your only relief is in hip-hop
So funk justice!

II

Twelve plus one
Was how it was done
When God sent his son
It was already won
And so it is
In a Media bliss
It happened like this
So why should it grab us?
Didn't they come and nab us?
Didn't they choose Barabbas?
Was it justice?
That a tree was found
Heaven turned upside down
He died outside of town
They washed their hands
Gave in to the crowd's demands
And then filled the stands
Watching like Roman do
Watch the gladiators who'
They've collected to murder you
Some disciples made the claim
They couldn't remember his name
They played this game
Saying they were not in his gang
I would've felt like using slang

On what tree will you hang?
How can you come to a bad end?
When you believed and you didn't pretend
But when they come you don't have a friend
And after you take their test
After you've given your best
And they've failed to make you confess
Make you give in to their ugliness
To send you to lockdown as their guest
That is their justice

III

Remember the day
James Earl Ray
Made Dr. King his prey
The man from the palace
Met cold blooded malice
And was killed in Dallas
Bobby not long
After that was gone
It's the same old song
So funk justice!
For national wealth
Safety and health
They'll put you to death
But your assassination
Is only a civil rights' violation
That's the price of annihilation
So funk justice!
When they accuse
Rhythm and blues
White socks and black shoes
Life can be hard to deal with
If you're not a Kennedy-Smith
You're not the American myth

And if the commentators explode
They can put your world in overload
And soon you're on the wrong road
If not for Liz
His place in showbiz
Would have ended in a fizz
And Mickey has his
Place forever at Walt Diz
And that's how it is
All you have is the Wiz
That's the vapor in the mist
That's the blindness of justice!

Chorus

You got to funk for the right to funk
You got to funk for the right to funk
Don't be a chump
Jump if you got to jump
Get over the hump
It's not that hard to jump
You got to funk for the right to funk
You got to funk for the right to funk

The End

Hooray for Justice

01/30/94

Every black person I have spoken with concerning Michael agrees that he had no choice but to buy his freedom. As long as others make the rules, and the law serves them and not us; we'll be faced with unfair dilemmas. The Press had already convicted him and he would have been crucified in court. Thank God it will never happen. Hooray for Michael! He bought justice.

I

They stood abreast
At parade rest
In a contest
To make the arrest
The message said at his address
Get him to confess
Dog him—give him no rest
It was a contest
For a hundred eighty days
But in this craving craze
The world got a glaze
At LA and Santa Barbara PD ways
Cops had to amaze
Working in a daze
Running them plays
They were in a panic for praise
It was as though
It was the Jack the Ripper's show
In business you never know

But business was never slow
The world had to know
And so they gave the world a show
And from the word go
Every morning there was this hello
Sorry but we don't know
When there will be an arrest
He has yet to confess
But we're giving him no rest
And we believe he will confess

II

It is a tragedy
Your majesty
And your attorney
Said it was all about money
Because of who you are—you see
In the land of the free
The opportunity
For fame and glory
Became a kid's story
And stalkers from the Press
Absolutely never rest
They will track down every address
Cops will do the rest
Put you to the test
They will undress
Make you vulnerable to the Press
But if there's nothing to confess
Why do they seem
Anxious to crush the dream
Of peace you wanted to redeem
They want to destroy your self-esteem
You're in this smoke stream
Like Dr. King you had a dream

You wanted love to reign supreme
But the way things seem
You're in an extreme
Get rich quick scheme
They don't care if you have no queen
They're gon' dog you out and treat you mean

III

With time to kill
The price is ten Mil
You have to cut a deal
But on the real
It doesn't matter how you feel
They will use overkill
And all your skill
Will go down if you chill
But when money has spoke
To the right folk
Pins will make the stroke
Your heart will not get broke
Oh how I choke
They're chopping at my oak
Still on that rope
They once killed our hope
But not this time
Rhythm and rhyme
Has paid the mighty dime
They can't declare a crime
Cash makes things sublime
You ringed that chime
You stepped to the line
You paid the fine
Your accusers have gone blind
Nothing is left behind
And justice is fine

She can stay blind
She took the money this time
With money there is no crime

IV

Some ask is it fair
Like they were there?
Do they really care?
Do they want to clear the air?
What about your share
In justice here
Can you escape the fear
Kill the smear
And still live here?
If you wanna know the deal
That's how I feel
Let's keep it real
They got ten mil
That's enough to kill
People for but still
Don't make me ill
He didn't kneel
He paid the dollar bill
The dollar controlled free will
So you see just like you
People do what they got to do
If you're rich enough it's true
You can use your IQ
You can buy up every clue
Money is more powerful than Voodoo
Hooray it's true
He did something most blacks cannot do
Now does that anger you?
Well tough! There is nothing you can do
But play catch thirty-two

And if that don't satisfy you
Know what I'm saying; screw you

Chorus

Hooray for justice
Even in the wrong
Money rights are strong
Hooray for justice
Hooray for justice
Money fights the wrong
Money rights are strong
Hooray for justice
Hooray for just us

The End

There Is No Justice For Us

01/30/94

I

And so the story
Says seeking glory
I know that roadie
He's Wild Bill Cody
Not the legend yes
But in the best
Almighty interest
Of some punk out west
In the course of time
The battle against crime
He joined the force
He tried to divorce
Michael from his rights
Come Saturday nights
He once put out the lights
Of pusher-parasites
But the game he was in
He was told was no win
So he took a tailspin
Went undercover again
Michael's case came up and he wanted in
He filled out his claim
The transfer came
He went after fame
To credit his name
He went out to get the king
Of pop and swing
One more thing

They took him to the ring
And showed him the probe
That they used to watch the globe
They wanted to disrobe
Michael like the devil did Job
That was the plot
It ran deep and hot
Then on the spot
They took the shot
Straight to Neverland
Questioned every woman and man
Like they had it in hand
Or so they told command
This undercover cop
Thought he had the drop
On the King of Pop
But wait a minute stop

II

If it's for justice
Just arrest us
Don't test us
Don't divest us
If God has blessed us
If he has confessed us
Why do you need to address us?
Why do you want to oppress us?
Michael was a slogan
It ran faster than Logan
Faster than the ex-Trojan
To the top and sure man
It was do or die
The reason why
It was for the apple pie
The good in good-bye

On television on "I-spy"
There was a funny guy
But a caging lie
Against a star from Gary
Is in the Rock Dictionary
It'd said he was legendary
That he was extra ordinary
King of Pop
On the drop
Wild Bill—the cop
Set his prop
He would opt
To bring down the King of Pop
Back to the hip-hop
I feel the finger pop
Didn't have the power
Though it came from every radio tower
And brought with it the midnight hour
And it hit like a meteor shower
But Wild Bill couldn't let go
He wanted everybody to know
That he'd stopped this Negro
It didn't happen like that though
But that's the way it goes
Against most Negroes
Why did these Jim Crows
Hate Michael so even his clothes?

III

Wild Bill had a rep
A rep to help
Late hours he kept
He hadn't slept
Since he began
This thing against this man

Who after Detroit Michigan
Became Peter Pan
And many fans feel
That he beat Wild Bill
When he cut the deal
He stopped the newsreel
They can't stop the flow
They can't defeat a hero
That they can't zero
And so Captain Nemo
The legendary King of Pop
Wild Bill failed to stop
This LA cop
This snap, crackle, pop
Broke a leak
MJ became a freak
The first week
They let the story leak
When it hit the scene
It was so low down and mean
It cost Michael a lot of green
Without a queen
He would be mobbed
His dignity robbed
You see on this planet of the apes
Where video tapes
Make or break a big time Lawyer
If he's hired by little Tom Sawyer
He can outdraw ya
And make it seem like he saw ya
He can call you a pedophile
And if he goes to trial
The racist media will smile
And in triple K style
A vicious dog
In court dialog
Will undress

This manifest
And if you fail any test
You will be subject to arrest

IV

And if some judge
With a grudge
Gets the urge
For hot fudge
And Wild Bill
Sent out there to kill
A superstar still
A star for real
In this world who is
A friend of his?
The legal way will persist
But money won't miss
Don't fall for the mirage
Don't face the charge
Go big and large
Use General George
With them dead presidents
And Washington's monuments
You can erase fingerprints
Because money represents
What Tyson didn't do
So I'm asking you
To do what you got to do
Like anybody else it happened to
After the LA quake
Everybody was awake
Waiting on something to break
Could it be a mistake?
Not according to us
Use "In God we trust"

There'll be no bust
So they'll have to stop their fuss
Tell media they can
Stop dogging my man
Now back to the band
Give my man a hand
Like he got in Japan
From the yellow man
Your fellow man
I said hello man
The king will be back again
So the world is gon' spin
Money can make you win
When you see him again
He'll be back in the top ten
And you'll say about back then
That you knew he would win
And if he choose be king again

V

Still some say why
Would an innocent guy
Let his money fly
Like birds to the sky
If he wasn't that way
Why did he pay?
But we don't know hey
The cops around LA
The ugly way
They did MJ
Almost every day
Calling the DA
With nothing to say
Except we're gon' put him away
He had to pay

He had to buy that play
Before this you see
They talked about J C
That wasn't groovy
But it became a movie
And so you deal
Or Wild Bill will
Use that overkill.
In Hollywood what's real?
Pictures are the things
Remember in King of Kings
When a body swings
Everybody sings
The same old tune
It's just a cartoon
That you see in your living room
Now don't assume
Because high noon
Was shot by the man in the moon
Mike knew the deal
He had to wait for Holyfield
But first he had to yield
To a man like Wild Bill
Who put him behind the walls of steel
Mike should've made a cash deal
Instead he let free will
Put him where he couldn't use his skill
So in conclusion
Beyond confusion
Money is a powerful allusion
It can stop that intrusion
Make Justice an illusion
It can get you the right conclusion

Chorus

There is no justice for us
Who would you trust
If it's you they come to bust
There is no justice for us
Who would you trust
If it's you they come to bust
There is no justice for us
Who would you trust
If it's you they come to bust
You'd trust in God we trust
You'd trust in God we trust
There is no justice for us

The End

Support Michael J.

Undated

I

Because of vices
A son of Isis
Who is the nicest
Is in a crisis
He's been accused
He's been used
He's been confused
Being the accused
It's all over the evening news
Investigators looking for clues
White socks and black shoes
Once a leader in rhythm and blues
Resolved after the J5 cruise
But he didn't stop
He became the King of Pop
A title that meant he was on top
But his popularity is starting to drop
Excuse my hip-hop
I'm simply pulling out all the stops
You see I still don't believe the cops
Can get the drop
On the King of Pop
And so I opt
To give him my support
To build for him a fort
To stop this cut throat
Efforts to sink his boat
The question is will shit float?

How long will it be so cut throat?
How long will he be their scapegoat?
I give him my oath
That I won't be remote
I'm going on report
As one speaking in his defense
Rapping to convince
You of his innocence
Use your common sense
He's not just singer—he's a prince
His wealth is immense
And though the situation is tense
Don't be overcome by the suspense

II

There comes a time you hate
And may be even debate
The unfairness of fate
But when they come straight
You make them wait
It's about the pieces of eight
The cost of media freight
If he refuses to be a lightweight
Will it make him less black?
He'll never ask for the money back
He deserves a fresh track
Not the arrogance of a media attack
So I'm rapping for that
They can't railroad this cat
I'm down like that
I smell the rat
I understand this act
He's too top hat
Some couldn't handle that
That's where they're at

His accusers want his Jack
They were willing to stab him in the back
Black must be about black
Though the pigmentation he may lack
Though Cali is warm and Spanish and old
But if you can feel you feel the white cold
Reaching out for your soul
So my choice is to be bold
About the thirteen year old
His folks were after gold
Desecrating a great soul
They wanted to control
Their futures and their goal
Was to get a fat bankroll
Enough to give them control
They wanted to take that stroll
So after the Super Bowl
They created this black hole
But before you take a poll
You should behold
The glitter of gold
That he paid was because he could not fold
Other than that the truth will never be told

III

In the San Fernandez Valley
In the state we call Cali
Where politicians go to rally
Where concrete walls form the alley
It's not hard to understand
They don't want a black Peter Pan
Who lives in Neverland
Of whom I am a fan
He is the King of Pop
And that they can't stop

So they send some cop
To try to get the drop
But you must understand
To me he's my main man
I feel like a member of his clan
I have always followed his band
I have always loved the man
I have always been a fan
And so I believe in the man
The man from Neverland
And like a member of the band
I accept his command
So I'm busting this verbal cap
To create a comprehendible gap
One day I will be on the map
What they are saying is crap
With all the smudging
And the begrudging
The lying and fudging
How can he get a fair judging?
Right now I'm urging
Him to keep submerging
Take the settlement
Tell the media to go get bent
They don't represent
The truth about us in print
They want a field day
They want to crucify MJ
But they can put them knives away
Because he will pay
And pay right away
And calling him gay
Won't make the difference okay
He will not be their prey

Bridge

Support Michael J.—Support Michael J.—Do you hear
what I say

Support Michael J.—Support Michael J.—Do you hear
what I say

Do you hear what I say—Support Michael J.—Support
Michael J.

Support Michael J.—Support Michael J.—and do it right
away

The End

Professional Merit

Every time I've seen Michael on stage he was a prince. He gave his absolute all to his audience and no one ever left feeling cheated. In those few interviews that he has allowed, he has done them with grace, calm and dignity. Obviously he wasn't born a monarch, but he has acquired monarch status. He has classic manners and he is extremely polite. Above all else, he is very professional. He was devoted to his fans and his fans were devoted to him. There was no heaven or hell on his stage, no promise of eternal joy or of eternal threat. It was all in the ecstasy of the moment.

His genius had redefined the way music videos would be done. Every one of his productions was like a short movie. I know it took a great deal of money to produce them maybe other artist couldn't afford that I don't know but after 'Thriller' the great videos had to have that extra dimension. Still his music was more than about song and dance; it was about social issues, which he handled beautifully. In fact no one handled that kind of subject matter as good as he did whether it was about gangs or race he was incredible.

I'm An Entertainer

Undated

I

You ask me why and it's very clear
Why I love my fans year after year
I can depend on them they're always there
They've always shown me they care
They've helped me overcome my fear
There is something we share
It could be as simple as a feeling
When my head is really reeling
And I'm on stage dealing
They give me a good feeling
They say: "Michael we love you"
All I can do is say I love you too
And God knows it's true
And they know I do
Because they feel it too
The whole world knows it's true
You can't hide that on stage
So when I come out I engage
Repressed feelings with rage
And as I turn that page
The stage comes to life
For years the stage was like a wife
When it cuts like a knife
I don't worry because that's my life

II

I breakdown and I scream
Like Dr. King I had a dream
In it love ruled supreme
It came to me like steam
My temperature would rise as I hit the floor
And when I realized that power I didn't fear anymore
Out there was the crowd and I controlled the show
I felt so proud and I knew where my life would go
My fans have given me everything
They have even called me their king
I'm a performer and I never played them cheap
I've made promises that I intend to keep
As long as I'm on my feet
As long as I can feel the beat
And feel what I feel when I feel the groove
As long as I can feel it I will move
Until I'm one with the groove
Although I've got nothing to prove
I am serious about my life and the way I live
And I still got a lot to give
The feeling inside keeps me hot
Cold is simply something I'm not
My fans have given me all I've got
And for them I'm taking this shot

III

I moonwalk and never leave the ground
I laugh and talk but I don't mess around
I'm serious about getting down
I make love to the world through sound
So don't unless you know where I've been
You don't have to be a friend
But if you stand against me stand to the end

Like any man I have sinned
But don't stop me because if you did
You would stop a dream that is never hid
Sometimes I might pause
And I do but not because
I've broken any laws
Don't scratch me with your claws
Or judge me because you have flaws
I do what I do because
It's what I choose to do
I'm trying to share my feelings with you
Love is too often not enough and always overdue
But there is nothing wrong with me loving you
So I dance and I try to make things feel all right
I try to love in that light
I stretch out and I care
And if you're near I'll try to take you there

IV

Time moves too fast as I've said to live in doubt
You have to forget the past if the past can't help you out
You have to live for the future and so I shout
When I feel the spirit I turn the place out
I love with all my heart and nearly all my soul
God knows that entertaining others is my goal
Like a preacher who preaches from days of old
Like a teacher who teaches you how to control
I have done all I could to prove my love is true
And it feels really good when I get it from you
There's nothing I wouldn't do for my fans and I know
I will never-never-never let them go
Even if I'm beaten to the ground
It will be because I'm trying to turn things around
I'm doing everything I can to help my fans get down
They are my fans and as long as my voice has sound

I will sing for them as I have since Motown
I did not ask for but I do accept the crown
And I accept what you have given me tonight
I love you all 'cause you make feel me all right
I feel good and I feel especially good tonight
I believe the expression for that is out of sight
So I thank you with all my heart and might
And I pray that God will bless all of you tonight

Bridge

I've put an attorney on retainer
Because I'm just an entertainer
I'm just a singer and a dancer
I have never tried to answer
The great questions of our time
Except to say to the world that I'm
Available to help any good cause
And I'm willing to pause
And I have in my career
And I do for sick children everywhere
Who I want to know that I am aware
That regardless of what happens here
I care and will never turn my back on that
No matter what's going on or where I'm at

The End

I Got the Feeling

Undated

I

I have been a volunteer
Each and every year
Since nineteen sixty eight
I've been a heavy weight
I have fought on and off stage
I've been on front page
And with pure emotion
I have given my devotion
With every step I've made
I've been true to the trade
I've sacrificed many times
And never forgot my lines
I've been there for you
Always my heart's been true
You have shown me love
True to the one glove
So I thank you tonight
For making me feel all right
I thank you for being there
And for showing me you care

II

I feel music in my soul
I'm living with one goal
And that's to turn you on
About that I feel strong
For twenty five years

The screams and cheers
Have helped me to rise
Many times in your eyes
I've been down but you've been fair
You've always shown me you care
And I know deep inside
That you have given me a special pride
I can stand because of you
That feeling allows me to do what I do
And I would like to say
When I'm down you make me feel okay
I thank you for being you
I thank you for being true
God knows I do love you
From the bottom of my heart I thank you

III

Honestly I really feel
Like breaking down for real
My heart is overfilled
And I'm so thrilled
To be with you tonight
You make me feel all right
Now if you feel the beat
Please get on your feet
It's all right tonight
It's all right because it feels all right
So get up if you can
You have made me a happy man
Happy to have so many friends
So many fans my head spins
Because I'm blessed so
And I'm grateful you're at the show
You make me wanna sing and dance
And while I have the chance

I wanna thank you for filling the stands
I thank you for being such special fans

IV

I thank you for being you
I thank you for being true
God knows I do love you
And he knows how grateful I am for you
You've shown me you care
I thank you for being there
I thank you for letting me share
I thank you for a supporting atmosphere
I thank you my friends everywhere
One day my name will clear
I will out live this smear
And I will never forget to show you I care
Without your love and support I'm nothing
Just a rag doll full of empty stuffing
But with you I'm not afraid of the bluffing
What enemies do to me means nothing
I thank you for helping me to be myself
I thank you for getting me off of that shelf
If they take everything and I've nothing left
I'll have you and I'll feel good about myself

Bridge

I got it—I got it—I got the feeling
It's such a good-good-good feeling
I got it—I got it—I got the feeling
It's such a good-good-good feeling
You're the reason my life is thrilling
You're the reason my life is fulfilling

It's such a good-good-good feeling
You're the reason I got the feeling
It's such a good-good-good feeling
I got it—I got it—I got the feeling

The End

Superstar

Undated

I

Before the fire and danger
And all of this anger
We filled the arenas with praise
Those were his best days
Fans loved him with a craze
Still Michael had his ways
His own peculiarities
His own rarities
That in combination
With artistic creation
Made his competitors dread
He was miles ahead
And being singular in kind
In spirit and mind
He transcended the stage
With subtlety and rage
He met each occasion
With such persuasion
His simple oration
Made his fans into a nation
On this his field of conquest
He never seemed to rest
Once he starts to perform
He's the calm and the storm
His audiences are spellbound
Lost in a galaxy of sight and sound
Nothing topped the anticipation
Of a Jackson presentation

It is an orchestration
Of unbelievable skill and adulation

II

Since I was a young man
I have watched the Jackson clan
I have watched Michael become a man
I have never stopped being a fan
Is there anyone like him?
He's a precious priceless gem
Thoughtful, witty and trim
He is like a beautiful hymn
Millions seek after him
He is just as awesome in film
Yet beneath the glitter and gold
Is this pure and noble soul
That stands above the cold
He is relentlessly in control
He has latitudes of kindness
A tough single mind'ness
That keeps him at the top of his craft
He is a spiritual raft
And to some the draft
Of a musical John Shaft
For who people in encore stand
With the world in the palm of his hand
He is in sold out demand
He hails from Neverland
And he's a home run hitter
He's never bitter
He is the thriller
And he's a pillar
Of strength and energy
He's a king in his industry

III

I ask you have you ever seen him turn
Go out on stage and burn
The place down with excitement
With every moment on stage spent
Few have ever went
Away in disappointment
He's a credit to his race
And he is in first place
This comes from years of dedication
Years of sacrifice and determination
Years of never saying never
Of always getting it together
When the M.C. says here's Michael Jackson
Everyone knows they're seeing an icon
A legendary performer second to none
The moment he hits the stage he's getting it done
Is he worth the wait I ask you?
If you've seen him you know what he can do
How he can excite and dazzle you
Taunt and mesmerize you too
He can stop and spin on a dime
Never leaving you behind
As he moonwalks to the back of your mind
You have witnessed one of a kind
And when he leaves there is nothing to resent
So great is his strength
His shows never seem to have enough length
You wonder where the time went
And so in so many ways
He's on your mind for days
That's what I call the Michael craze
All I can do is give the man the praise

Chorus

He's a superstar performer—He gives you drama
He's a superstar performer—He relieves your trauma
He's a superstar performer—He's no bummer
His performances are supernormal—He's a superstar

The End

For-My-Fans

01/30/94

I

No one gave me the groove
I took it from every school
No one taught me how to move
It came from my gene pool
So I got nothing to prove
So what if they rule
That's not gon' change the way I move
Not gon' stop me from finding the groove
For over twenty years
I've tried to stop the tears
And through all the fears
I've listened to the cheers
And I've loved it for years
And for fans I've held back the tears
And I will overcome the new fears
Their love has kept me through the years

II

I'm not on an ego trip
My fans would really flip
And I'm not going to hip
My enemies to every slip
As though they give a rip
My fans and I have an important friendship
On that I'll never skip
I'm not about to slip
And fall for a fake again

I'll be careful the next time I choose a friend
And I'm not going to pretend
That I'm without sin
But I'm true in heart and will be 'til the end
This time I was taken
But I will be back even though I'm shaken
I will return to the top ten

III

Yes it took me by surprise
I just didn't realize
Hooked by compromise
And hurt so much by lies
Drugs did paralyze
Someone said that lies
Don't stand up in paradise
Put your trust in Christ
And evil won't destroy
I've done nothing but try to bring joy
For that I'm being used as a decoy
A plaything and a media toy
A scandal piece for some talk show
The darkness doesn't want to let go
But my fans all know
I would never stoop that low

Bridge

I'm gon' rock and roll to the end
And I will be careful the next time I choose a friend
I said rock and roll to the end
I said I'm gonna rock—I said I'm gonna rock—rock to the
    end

Rock for my-fans—for-my-fans—for-my-fans
I'm gonna rock and roll 'til the end
I'm gon' rock for my fans, for my fans, for my fans
I'm gonna rock and roll 'til the end

The End

Family Influence

Every family has one pied piper that plays a different tune; Michael's though an exceptional one is no exception. Greatly annoyed at Latoya's betrayal, in this chapter I have tried to address those feelings. I have also tried to be sympathetic although at times I've questioned why I wanted to keep such a balance. I believe it was out of my fondness of Michael, knowing how generous he is, I know she has hurt him but beyond initial reaction, I can't help believe he has forgiven her. The Jacksons are a quilt of strength and flexibility. They have all the features of a class monarch's family. There is strength, jealousy, calamity, joy, a great love for each other, and a sense of being special in a world where few black families are. They are greatly respected in the world of entertainment. As a black family to blacks they're immortalized. Even through betrayal their love for each other manages to always keep them intact. They know its role in history and they manage to measure up. This little brief flurry of verses tries to address and answer things that may or may not have been real, but if not, at the time I wrote them, the possibilities seemed strong.

Let me point out that the term 'little sister' does not refer to chronological age but family position. I apologize for often dealing perhaps too much with the issue of betrayal but at the time of consideration I was so overwhelmed with shock I found myself out of control so those feelings found form in my poetry. Still as I look at the high place the Jacksons occupy in my life I feel great humility that I have a gift that I can use to honor them especially Michael.

He Cut Her Loose

02/06/94

I

He controlled the juice
And he cut her loose
She cooked her own goose
I don't mean to sound obtuse
But to tell the truth
Like a bad tooth
He cut her loose
She was guilty of misuse
And photo abuse
She broke a family truce
He kicked back like Bruce
And he cut her loose
She lost her place to roost
She had no real excuse
The game was never deuce
He controlled the juice
And he cut her loose
Just like the god Muse
He was said to be a recluse
Maybe so but in her world he was Zeus
With music busting loose
She got the noose
But it was hers to choose
She had all of the clues
She knew her brother's views
And how much she could lose
She abandoned rhythm and blues
White socks and black shoes

But if you lit a fuse
To C-4 you expect the news
To have a certain amount of blues
But propaganda can confuse

II

On the front line yapping
Her habituation to photo snapping
Got her a financial butt slapping
And so I'm recapping
He probably thought she was lacking
But she was star tracking
But that's not the reason she had to get packing
That was because she lost his backing
And that's a shellacking
It's not computer hacking
After which she started counter attacking
The girl was lacking
She knew she would be
Punished for her nudity
Especially if it publicly
Embarrassed the family
She had been warned
But she had never earned
It would be a hard lesson learned
She would get burned
She was told to let the Playboy thing go
But she had to have her own show
I guess she thought she wouldn't really have to go
But he thought what she did was low
That's why I say yo!
She sold out to be a photo ho
A vampire you know
But a photo ho
Will never say so

And you won't know
Until the blood flow
So no matter where you go
If you see the photo
You should know the ho

III

If she was a guy
Or I was Princess Di
I'd punch her in the eye
What she says is a lie
She's just jealous
Of the fellows
And there's malice
But she wasn't Alice
In Wonderland not only was she jealous
She was also careless
First it was just Joe
When that got slow
She opened her Michael window
And the wind did blow
She hoped it would grow
Into a chance to go
On talk show after talk show
She didn't let any of her family know
It was a painful enterprise
For them to keep fighting her lies
Dealing with media spies
What she did is bad in my eyes
Her lies I despise
Yes she's a good looker
A video hooker
And so they took her
She thought they would book her
But when they did it was for only one show

For stuff about him they wanted to know
And she earned a little dough
But they didn't want a photo ho
Just what they think she'd know
So it became a thing of come and go
And before she realized it she melted away like snow

IV

Hey I don't play deuce
Screw Mother Goose
I'm busting loose
With the crazy ass truth
The girl was uncouth
A real Saber Tooth
Like High karate Bruce
I'm kicking back and busting loose
In Rocky and the Moose
Bull Winkle had the juice
Michael — the recluse
Like the mighty Zeus
Had the power and cut her loose
She was guilty of photo abuse
What about the news
Is it true all Jews
Have money and views?
But white socks and black shoes
Is strictly Rhythm and Blues
The girl had no moves
She made no grooves
And no one improves
Their funk without grooves
To tell the truth
She probably needed Dr Ruth
Anyone can see Michael cut her loose
This little gold egg laying goose

Tried to blow off the roof
But her stories weren't a hundred proof
I'm sorry honey you didn't have to goof
All you had to do was put it through the hoof
Instead he cut you loose
In your world he song like Muse but he was Zeus

Chorus

And though he's very recluse
Some say he's Muse
In her world he was Zeus
And he cut her loose
I understand it was for cash-dollars-ma'am
That everybody wants including Uncle Sam
But if it's family ma'am you give a damn
Or one day nobody will want you in the jam

The End

You Made 'em Go Joe

02/08/94

I

I'm not trying to trip
I can't spare the whip
I can't deal with the lip
If we go we're going from zip
The kingdom was under tension
Michael was near suspension
Under pressure I decided to mention
Standards were by convention
And the price has been paid
And hopefully public interest will fade
Yet you too can be betrayed
By an employee like a chambermaid
So I'm running over everything
Trying my best to protect my king
It'd been a long time since I'd heard him sing
Or saw him do that moonwalk thing
The one thing he has is distinction
And now he's threatened with extinction
So I would like to turn your attention
To another dimension
Joe was always tuff
He was a man of no bluff
Everybody knew he was show nuff
His family had caught it ruff
That means a hard way to go
He said now if we do a show
We have got to get a good score
We've got to give them more

Than anyone has before
Make them beg for an encore
He also said if we go
If we go we go with what we know
That means we go all out
Until they dance and shout
We have got to turn it out
There can be no doubt
As to what J 5 is about
So go out there and turn it out
Joe had that iron will
The boys had the skill
Motown had the deal
Joe Jackson was for real
As young as they were on stage
It became the Jackson Five Age
They could drive their fans to rage
They were constantly on front page

II

Now history as it was made
Saw that they got paid
They were the best in the trade
Michael would serenade
Leave the place smoking
Leave you heart broken
There was nothing token
About the J 5 open
As sure as arenas would fill
Fans could count on a thrill
The boys never had time to kill
There was always another drill
Another routine to learn
Every dollar they got they earned
They went out on stage and burned

The dividends had to return
From the very beginning
They came out winning
Young girls were grinning
But Joe permitted no sinning
No premarital sexual affairs
No girls ever went up those hotel stairs
They weren't just stars they were flares
When they ignited the world was theirs
I saw them in person twice
Michael was always nice
Always knew how to break the ice
He was born with the spice
He just had so much taste about him
No one who knew him could doubt him
Everybody talked about him
Even before he left them
He was different in some way
The world would see that one-day
As children they never had time to play
And I guess that wasn't okay
But no one thought about it back then
We didn't know 'til they became men
And that was an awful sin
But they were so great then
Sometimes you hurt within
But they were great and they did win

III

First of all it's past tense
So it don't make sense
For me to convince
You of Joe's relevance
His contributions are immense
He was the fence

That protected their innocence
Yes he was intense
His boys were gon' be somebody
Joe didn't believe in doing nothing shoddy
And he gave that pride to his kids
No egos or ids
Got in Joe's way
Joe was there night and day
Teaching them how to play
Making sure there would be a payday
A future for them one day
Thank you Joe for showing them the way
When they took to the road
Joe carried the load
Maybe he did explode
It was a mighty heavy load
To have on board
Joe was no toad
No kiss to download
Somewhere down the road
He was the warrior who did it right
Night after night after night
Until they were out of sight
They practiced every night
He taught them though he got uptight
They never faltered under the spotlight
They made the world seem bright
Each one of them a royal knight
Only a fool can't see
What Joe has done for music history
And through his sons did it magically
Thank Joe for it was he
That gave them the chance to be
The famous J 5 company
So you see automatically
He's all right with me
In fact out of sight with me

They made me feel free
And it makes me angry
Seeing people give Joe the third degree

IV

I remember Vietnam
And how we use to jam
Before a body slam
Serving Uncle Sam
We took the combat exam
And we didn't give a damn
As long as we could jam
Knowing we would leave the Nam
Motown kept it real for me
Kept bringing back a positive reality
It was "one two three it's easy
That's how easy love can be"
That put me beyond that jive
Motown sound kept me alive
I wanted to survive
And see the Jackson Five
So thank you Joe thank you
And thank Katy too
You did what you had to do
People should be thanking you
For what you all gave us
Michael one day still may save us
From those who would enslave us
Mark and engrave us
Those who exploit that "I own you behavior"
Know Michael could be the savior
Because he's such a good neighbor
And many seek his favor
He's deserving of our trust
Instead of the disgust

The talk and the fuss
He's been receiving from us
I don't mean to deviate
But if you concentrate
Michael's debt was paid
Before he left first grade
He gave his body and soul
Long before Control
And Janet reached gold
She used him as a mold
I don't feel sorry for Latoya
Remember I told ya
She will bore ya
Musically she can't score for ya
She was never a choice
The girl has no voice
This talk about little boys
Is another way of shooting decoys
But you know I must confess
As far as the Press
Is concerned and the rest
Of the vultures in this mess
They knew she was mad
Long before "I'm bad"
She hated Michael and her dad
One of them made her leave the pad
So now she is downing Michael too
Making his fans boohoo
That's such an obvious thing to do
I guess she is in phase 2
But as long as the sky is blue
We know what she says is untrue
It's hurting me too
How can it be true?
Some people can't see because the Elvis they knew
Isn't like Janet, the others or you Michael in my view

Chorus

You made 'em go Joe—You made 'em go—Hey! Yo!
You made 'em go Joe—You made 'em go—Hey! Yo!
You made 'em go Joe—You made 'em go—Hey! Yo!
You made 'em go Joe—You made 'em go—Hey! Yo!
So thank you Joe—Thank you—You made 'em go
Thank Katherine too oh—Thank both of you—I thank
      you so
You made 'em go Joe—You made 'em go—Hey! Yo!
You made 'em go Joe—You made 'em go—Hey! Yo!

The End

It Don't Stop

Undated

I

Now ain't you hipped?
Tito got whipped
Then Joe found out he could cook
He could make book
It was over a broken guitar string
That Joe found out they could sing
And they could swing
And they could really do that thing
And when Michael turned it on
The Jackson Five was born
And though worn and torn
From going to school and getting it on
They did the bars
Instead of washing cars
These boys became stars
But there would be scars
It took discipline and pain
Lost childhood sustained
And they maintained
For one day they would entertain
And one would become a king
He would teach the world to sing
He would make the world swing
He came from the J 5 thing

II

Gary was a dirty steel town

People were poor for miles around
But they loved to get down
Most of them on the Motown sound
Michael copied James Brown
And saw Jackie Wilson and found
A way to spin and turn around
They were destined for Motown
After they sang and played loud
And won that Apollo crowd
Which made their mother proud?
They could no longer be hidden by the cloud
Of dust over Gary—They had found exposure
Barry Gordy in an exclusive disclosure
Said we're signing them today
From then on they were on their way
When they moved to LA
The whole world met MJ
His brothers were just as good
Behind him they always stood
Beside him they always would
They were blessed and they were good
But he was special from the start
And soon would win the world's heart

III

After accomplishing their dreams
Things happened it seems
Just like Diana left the Supremes
Michael too had different dreams
His first solo album as I recall
Was "Off The Wall"
It did okay but was small
Compared to the greatest hit of all
Which like a fairy tale
Made him the world's most popular male

He swept the world in a gale
He broke the all time record sale
The album was a killer
It was called "The Thriller"
It sold fifty eight million plus
Michael said he did it for us
And then as a Superstar must
He formed a world trust
Dedicated to saving this planet
Shortly afterward his sister Janet
Carried her own moon beams home in a jar
And emerged as the next Jackson Superstar
But Michael was king
Of the world of swing
Everyone paid to hear him sing
And proclaimed him as the king

Bridge

After the Jackson Five
Michael came alive
He would survive
And would arrive
As the King of Pop
It don't stop—He's the King of Pop
Give him his prop
He's the King of Pop
Give him his prop
It don't stop—He's the King of Pop

The End

But That's Okay

02/13/94

I wanted to take a look at why Latoya blessed extraordinarily well, would seemingly jeopardize it all. Although it was imaginative, I developed a good model upon which to draw inference, and perhaps, at least for myself, come close to a reason why a little rich girl would turn on her own family, so viciously. Why did she become a family outcast? Why did she develop that "It's better to rule in hell than serve in heaven?" attitude?

I

The way it started
She was broken hearted
Maybe not regarded
She felt discarded
Why wasn't she started
When Michael departed?
Her act an act retarded
She should've been rewarded
Janet had had her Good Times
But came back to the rhymes
Presenting her lines
In Rhythm Nation Times
You see Joe chose Janet
To send to the planet
When he did a little pomegranate
Heart turned hard as granite
She couldn't stand it

She didn't land it
She turned bandit
Now understand it
Just like the Titanic
She caused a great panic
The Jacksons were authentic
But she was frantic
Joe had promoted Janet
To be second on the planet
And if Michael said okay
Daddy have it your way
It was a brand new day
But she didn't see it that way
She grew angry with MJ
And all he did if he did say
Was in time little sister hey
I'll help you but not today
So frustration made its play
Turned her that very day
Set her against MJ
And keeping up I know
I imagined this even so
First she tried to do Joe
Because really though
Joe had made things go
He was the guy Yo!
Behind the famed Jackson Five Show
He was the one that made them all go
Heart broken she started hating Joe
He was daddy the hero
And he had hurt her so
Though she carried the family name
She had no personal fame
There was nothing she could claim
And what a shame
She ran her game
Anything to get in lights her name

Michael was off in Europe someplace
Though he had little do with her case
That didn't erase
Her hatred was in place
And it had a deep base
It was something he too would have to face

II

Every thought in her brain
Brought back pain
But the acquisition of fame
Is a numbers game
You must have fans to reign
Should I explain
To have the fame
Of the Jackson name
You got to entertain
It's "no pain no gain"
And certainly no champagne
It took a celebration
To release her frustration
After Rhythm Nation
She plunged into a kind of preoccupation
She wanted her own name up in lights
Her own contract rights
How many family fights
And how many non-invites
Would she have to go through
Before she was recognized too?
She had to do what she had to do
After all she was a Jackson too
And it was time the world knew
That she had talent too
So from the family she withdrew
And went out to do her thing too

It was a hard thing for a young girl
Who had lived in her brother's world
In finery like a Duchess of Earl
Finally destiny had unfurled
And she was not to be
The new star in the family
Thinking "How could this happen to me"
Her superstar brother and her daddy
Had failed her, she hated them deeply
"They could have made me"
Ran through her mind like a bad movie
They had become the enemy
The pressure was too great
Any consideration too late
She was consumed with hate
She left the Jackson estate
Vowing to take revenge on them
Especially on him
As a wounded seraphim
Her future looked dim
Compared to rest of them
It was all because of him
He was the family's gem
She wanted to hurt them
So after her father she turned on him
She thought in her mind screw them
Now that's hard to understand
How do you turn on a man?
A man who is like a black Peter Pan
Do you do it just because you can?
Just because you don't have fans
But when evil lands
It don't count hands
Unfortunately it consumes and expands

III

So when not promoted
She became devoted
It should be noted
She was out voted
So she broke it
Went family-phobic
Became dark and anaerobic
When Janet spoke it
"What have you done for me lately"
She thought they must hate me
Why didn't they make me?
Instead they forsake me
Joe misread every clue
And really never knew
His little girl was untrue
To Jackson values 'til she did her do
Until she joined the human zoo
You know it's true
People who do you too
Are close like that to you
They never say boo
They just work that voodoo
Until it works on you
And working it on through
Michael it's up to you
What you gon' do?
She's your sister too
So I'm asking you
Are you gon' do her too?
Screw her because she tried to screw you?
You should've backed her too
Let her travel with you
Then she could've left her husband who'
Belongs in the zoo

If only I knew
Some ancient juju
Some Shaka Zulu
I could have ended her reign of voodoo
Otherwise it's up to you
To give her a review
She's in your heart too
So is your heart true
Doesn't God live there too?
So what are you going to do?
With Janet's busting loose
Filled with Jackson juice
She does the boogaloo
Just like you do
But unlike you and Janet
This one will never make the Daily Planet
Unlike superstar-boy and girl
Who have rocked the world
What can this one do?
She has lost her Cinderella shoe
Trying to get even with you
What are you going to do?
The world is watching you
After what you've been through
Will you hurt her too?
Abandon her on "Paid For View"

IV

So why do you doubt?
I know she's no Girl Scout
But she's been left out
No crowds to shout
Little sister turn the muthda out
With little doubt
She's had her pain

No one to entertain
Or recognize her claim to fame
The family name
Couldn't sustain
Her I want to be somebody too pain
In falsehood she seemed to gain
At least recognition again
Otherwise she was watching the rain
Fall on an expensive windowpane
Looking at the world
Wondering why wasn't she the girl?
The family's Duchess of Earl
That perfect pearl
She had the name
But no right to the fame
Oh what a shame
She'd staked her claim
On the Jackson name
In a way that would defame
Now she may never earn her name
So for what should she aim?
She was filled with shame
Someone had to be the blame
It's always the same
"You could've help me too
She thought: "I'm Jackson like you
I can do what Jacksons do
And I trusted you
I trusted father too
I've stayed with mama all my life
But mama is his wife
His helping Janet was a knife
By right my life
Should have been in the Daily Planet
Instead he chose Janet
She had had another career
I waited for my year

It never got here
It's perfectly clear
All of you turned on me
They paid handsomely
For my nudity
You didn't rescue me
I exercised my free will
But still your power to kill
Left me with no deal
I thought how can this be real?
So how should I feel
When everything for me is unreal?
I never had a chance
To sing and dance
Not like the others
Janet, you and my other brothers"

V

Guess you might say
She upped and ran away
Thinking every dog has its day
But if you can't play
Turn night to day
On stage they say
Sorry that's okay
Come back another day
She couldn't sing
And didn't swing
In the center ring
She didn't have the family's thing
She was dangling on a string
Watching Michael's reign
She was in a one-girl sorority
Where her lack of royalty
Under Joe's authority

Caused her to lose her loyalty
She felt betrayed by the sovereignty
She was a novelty
Without the talent
She wasn't gallant
Nor a princess at the ball
No not that at all
Just a girl on call
That girl down the hall
And you know after all
Shortly after "Off the Wall"
She took Playboy's call
Which set up her fall
They made her the centerfold
Photographed her naked soul
And that wasn't her goal
But after Janet's had Control
All Thriller had really sold
The others were getting old
Waiting on a J 5 return
In Hell you burn
If you don't learn
If unluckily you earn
A woman's scorn
It could make you wish you hadn't been born
Suddenly there was a scandal
That meant a house to vandal
She was a burnt out candle
Because you didn't handle
A childhood broken heart
Your judgment wasn't smart
And now it could tear your world apart
You gave her no start
And showed little regard
For her broken heart
She played her part
But got no music award

So back to the start
Michael you are known for your heart
How do you like hurt?
It's just common dirt
She throwing—she went a little berserk
Which is easy to do in your line of work

Chorus

But that's okay—It's okay—It's okay
But that's okay—It's okay—It's okay
All you got to say is that's okay—it's okay
Michael you must forgive her one day
But that's okay—It's okay—It's okay
But that's okay—It's okay—It's okay
All you got to say is that's okay—it's okay
Michael you must forgive her one day

The End

I'm Sorry Little Sister

02/14/94

I

I'm sorry little sister don't worry
I guess I've been in too much of a hurry
I never knew that we were hurting you
And believe me I'm hurting too
I never thought I was ignoring you
I must've forgot you needed adoring too
The times we lost are gone
I know you can't live in this world alone
I guess I recognize that now
We should get together somehow
Maybe we can't forget everything
I know its hard because it's hard to sing
When in your soul you've felt such pain
But I want us to be a family again
And that's gon' take understanding all the way round
I'm not here to try to put you down
But if you love me like I love you
We can do this together and not put each other through
More difficulty than we have to
I want you to know I'm thinking of you

II

You know I believe in family
And I forgive you for hurting me
And I'm saying it publicly
Because sister we are family
Nothing can change that in my view

I'm hurting sister just as bad as you
And I want this over too
Because after everything said I love you
And always will feel the same
We share more than our name
I didn't understand 'til I felt this shame
And saw the pain in this game
Though we may not always agree
We can work it out as a family
All it takes is you loving me
And me loving you with eyes that see
I'm saying there's been enough misery
And we don't need to keep it company

III

I know you've said mean things
Sometimes the anger bell rings
I know you've said I was strange
Still I want things between us to change
I really care about you
It's hard living without you
God forgives us for the wrong we do
And in that light I forgive you
All it takes is your hand in mine
And the promise that we will combine
Our energies and work it out over time
For the good of the rhythm and the rhyme
As a family we've always been strong
And as a family we can overcome wrong
That's why our family's spirit lives on
But like us it can't survive alone
So let's leave the bad in the past
And work together to make our love last

IV

You see if you got a strong loving family
No prison can keep you from being free
No talk alone can destroy me
I'll understand if you don't want to be
Associated but you can trust me
My gift to you is my love for you—don't you see
Our love is why there's no other family quite like us
Though we argue, fight and fuss
We are all part of one family trust
Standing behind each other for what's ahead of us
Little sister I'm telling you
I couldn't see and I never knew
That the family was hurting you
I guess I looked but saw no clue
Now in great personal pain I'm clearing my mind
I promise you I'll never again be so blind or unkind
The one thing we'll always have is each other
I love you and I'll always be your brother

Ad Lib

You got to live little sister you got to live
You got to give little sister you got to give
So let's forgive little sister and try to live
All we got is our love and love can forgive
And that God's will little sister that his will
And that God's will little sister that his will
If you give you'll be forgiven that's his will
Nothing can hurt us under his loving will

Chorus

And you got to deal with that and you got to live with that
    and
You got to deal with that and you got to live with that and
    you
Got to deal with that and you got to live with that and you
    got
To deal with that and you got to live with that
And that's where it's at you got to deal and live with that
And you got to deal with that and you got to live with that
    and
You got to deal and you got to live with that

The End

Talking About Latoya and Paranoia

02/16/94

I

He was forgiving
But it's hard living
Where everybody has a name
And you don't have a claim
You're nothing to the fame
And all you feel is shame
Why aren't you in the game?
You waited but your chance never came
False images appear in your brain
You can't maintain
They're driving you insane
You always complain
That's your campaign
Your brother's the acclaim
Main man with the Jackson name
But he doesn't feel your pain
He left you on a plane
For a life on the stage
That he started at a young age
They beg for him but no one begs for you
But what can you do?
He says he's trying to save you
He probably is from you being you
He doesn't want to sacrifice you too
And in your heart you know it's true
But for what do you ask
You say: you can handle the task
And that you're ready at last

But time is fleeing fast
You asked: "So when will I go?
And when will I know?
And when will I have my own show?
Daddy says he doesn't know"
You're too easy to depress
You wanna change your address
Your anger grows deeper
Are you your brother's keeper?
You could call his personal beeper
But that would make you feel cheaper
You feel cheated
You feel depleted
You feel mistreated
You're completely defeated
Living on family money
Wanting to be a Bunny
But your brother says no
He won't let you go
But what does he know
You have got to have your own show
With a sister with Control
Who is reaching her goal
All you're getting is old
In anger you sell your soul

II

Nobody knew nor could they know
That you would sell out for a photo
Become a part of Playboy's portfolio
Though your brother told you no
"Wait sister you know
That's not the way to go"
He gave you whatever you ask for so
If he said no he meant no

But you had to go
The rest is history yo!
You became a photo ho
Attacked your father yo
But that got you a zero
You will never be a hero
The good book says honor your father
But that was such a bother
No wonder your brother
Talked about you to your mother
I mean really though
You're not even a pro
Like the others in your family no
You're just a photo ho
Black widow sister yo!
And you don't even have a show
So your final solution
Was to destroy your family as a great institution
Michael doesn't know it but he's a substitution
For your father and so you sought retribution
You started to slang smut
Somebody should've kicked your little butt
All you do is deal in hurt
All you dig up is dirt
You broke family laws
You're a traitor to the cause
You're not perfect because you have flaws
You ought to stop and pause
Turn around and look again
Your brother might be thin
But he's heavy from within
Show me a man without sin
Don't you see you're hurting his heart?
Don't you see you're tearing it apart?
'Cause he gave you no start
Girl you'd better get smart
You're living on the run

Not knowing where you're going
Or what you're doing?
You're playing with a loaded gun?
Afraid to go out in the sun
Living in the darkness can't be fun
But here's how it really is
If you're not a friend of his
You're just another rabbit to chase
They only want you for a taste
Come on girl look into my face
How can you profit from disgrace?

III

It was your father's choice
Like it was with the boys
You had no voice
And you say no choice
Except the silver spoon
In your mouth before noon
You're running like a mad coon
Slobbering at the moon
You have exercised your right
Became a photo ho overnight
You did it all for spite
Or did it suit your appetite?
You took the first strike
Telling your family to take a hike
It was a venomous trick
Bitten you were obviously sick
You turn nobody on
Said you were left home alone
At least you had a home
From here to Rome
You're out there and you trying to kill
Your brother's rep by spreading ill will

You just don't have the skill
But there's blood to spill
Is it worth that to be on top?
And seemingly you can't stop
Like a trigger-happy cop
Until you hear the gun pop
Or they rule you insane
Until then you're in the game
You're in the center lane
Trying to make a name
But you're just a photo ho
On every TV talk show
Do they want you I say no?
They want what they think you know
That's the reason you're on any show
And then away you go
You're hurting people who love you—don't you know?
You're like a played out old picture show
He carried you for years
You should be in tears
Instead of promoting smears
Out there throwing spears
But you're running out of time
You've got no rhythm and rhyme
And your other crime
Is that you're dealing with slime
Against your own family
Supplying the enemy
In radio and on TV
Girl you ain't no sister to me

IV

On a road to scandal
Your career you vandal
Now who will handle

This burnt out candle?
A threat to the throne
Like an Armageddon
You're the onslaught
And learning naught
What good have you brought?
And when you get caught
In the ugly afterthought
For the hurt you have brought
With the lies you sold
For thirty pieces gold
You won't have your sister's Control
And it'll rip out your soul
And when no one cares anymore
And you got nothing left to score
Living out the drug store
And dead for sure before
You receive the last rights
After the drug fights
And that crazy husband nights
Punching out your lights
By then you'll be all dried up
Drinking from a bitter cup
The same cup you're giving everybody
Well I'm sorry Miss Claudie
But that's no way to party
What you're doing isn't for the hardy
It's just for the heartless
The spiritless and artless
You better ask somebody
'Cause in a dream I don't see anybody
As the hearse pulled in
I don't see a friend
Just a guy real thin
Standing there—Michael J. to the end
It's talent if you don't have it
Don't try to grab it

Let someone else have it
Don't be a carrot for the rabbit
That's a bad habit
And please don't be the rabbit
There are some things you just can't do
And your family has to put up with you
Those friends now in the end won't say boo
They won't even remember you
You'll be out of the family's trust
If asked what have you done for us
They will say she's not one of us
You'll be another one bites the dust
Girl—stop going around
Putting your brother down
Don't you recognize this is a hanging?
A black star gangbanging
Another leader destroyed
The one we all have most enjoyed

Chorus

Talking about Latoya and paranoia!
Talking about Latoya and paranoia!
Talking about Latoya and paranoia!
Talking about Latoya and paranoia!
We all have seen it:—paranoid schizophrenic
We all have seen it:—paranoid schizophrenic
Talking about Latoya and paranoia!
Talking about Latoya and paranoia!

The End

He Ain't No Suspect

02/18/94

I was reluctant to do another rap on Latoya's talk show follies, but she just won't go away; and she was a creditable threat to Michael. Why didn't they ask her since she seemed concerned for sexually abused children, did she donate money to help them? I was really sick of her spitefulness and of that blood sucking talk show host pimping her like a forty-dollar ho.

I

On another talk show
The same little Jacko
Launched another attack
Knifed her brother in the back
While leader of the pack
Kept the show on track
He must be asking: "What's wrong wit' her Mama
What she's doing is a bummer
Causing all of this trauma
I don't need the drama, Mama
I knew she wasn't smart but is she really dumber?
Do you have her number?
Look! It's starting to thunder
I got to go but I wonder"
My guess is only her husband can say
Why she's attacking MJ?
She got no talent anyway
She has money but not enough okay
Now what is a husband

If he ain't your man
And maybe no man
Has had his hands
In those underpants
But if you want to be advance
If you really wanna dance
Then give the king a chance
He can fill the stands
What's a normal romance?
She doesn't have sex
Is that a complex?
And if it is how's she talk?
She should take that bull and walk
But before she does wake up the help
Let's get ourselves in step
Look there's no gravity
In what she says to me
Her spouse is an abuser
And she is a sore loser
And may be a boozer
Why did he choose her?
He wanted Jackson money
Well thank you Honey
Connect me to Sony
This girl is a phony
She can't sing
She can't swing
Can't do a damn thing
But wear a punk's wedding ring

II

I'm back with the fog
Checking out my monologue
You talk show dog
Do you feel like a frog?

You try to junk
My main man punk
Check out my funk
That baud's a drunk
Let me do you a story
One about Miss Glory
One about the mandatory
Whiteness of her territory
Your little Jacko got no name
Except her Jackson claim
And without her Jackson name
You wouldn't have her this case is frame
Don't even talk about it
How can you doubt it?
Or believe anything she say
About sweet MJ?
Just ain't no way
She's looking for a payday
If you didn't wanna know
About him on your show
Would have some little photo ho?
She would have nowhere to go
She says she's got records overseas
They must be played on foreign keys
May be they are with the monkeys
I mean you know please
Show me she's not a tease
She may have a mental disease
But you know what's going on
Don't you punk—you're wrong
She's out here alone
And soon her money will be gone
And when that happens you won't phone
You want to destroy the throne
And once it's gone you'll leave her alone
But we aren't gon' stand
By and let you destroy my man

One day MJ will have command
Until then the forces of Neverland
Are willing to die
To protect the guy
'Cause he's the most
Nicest guy on the coast
And that's no boast
That's why I'm on post

III

Wait-wait-wait—hello!
I've tried to be mellow
Like Old Dog Yellow
But I can't cut it fellow
He is not a slob
Don't need your job
He don't work for the mob
You the one need a job
Digging in the dirt
Causing this hurt
You're just a jerk
But that's how you work
That show's me how sick
Isn't this the land where Tricky Dick
Did the Watergate trick
He got away with it didn't he Slick?
Put that under your hat
But you don't talk about that
Or the Iran Contra act
Like that ain't fact
So get off my man's back
Find someone else to attack
He's rich and he's black
Is that why your bloodhounds are trying track
Still anything goes

Against Negroes
Do you supposes
There are news pros
That are a little racist
That prefers white faces
Go to white only places
Promoting their Dick Tracies
Speaking of freaking
The cops were peaking
And strictly speaking
The story they were leaking
Is just a dirty lie
I don't believe it why
It's against a rich black guy
Who has a piece of the pie
Someone they could crack on
Try to get us to turn our hold back on
Promote a lie while he was in Rome
Michael, welcome back home
Do the brothers over there feel strong
Bout 'em over here doing you wrong?

Chorus

Cops should serve and protect—He ain't a suspect
Cops should serve and protect—He ain't a suspect
Cops should serve and protect—He ain't a suspect
He's a victim of this system of intolerance and neglect

The End

Come On Home

02/28/94

I

This is my second attempt
To reach you nymph
Your hurt ain't exempt
You're making me limp
Working off this smear
Instead of spreading fear
You should be spreading cheer
Making it another Michael year
That's what I'm doing here
One day his name gon' clear
As sure as Shakespeare
Could've said it I'm here
For another round for the crown
Take me downtown
And don't funk around
I wanna be there if Michael gets down
You been the host
Running like a ghost
From coast to coast
Now you got no post
No post to piss on
And no place to roam
Once Michael gets home
If home ain't gone
He'll be back on the throne
But a lot of hope will be gone
We're not gon' let him face this alone
Can you make it on your own?

Yeah the jealousy you got
Keeps you keeping it hot
So you take another cheap shot
Trying to screw up our Camelot
You're not the one in command
But you're out there attacking the man
What hope can you give Neverland?
You know what I'm saying?
What hope have you for the black man?
Can't you see the evil tricks you're playing?
You're mature but you're acting like a little girl
Secondly you're not a Duchess of Earl
How dare you rock our world
And why have you hurled
Yourself upon Michael's galaxy
Like it's where you're supposed to be?
Michael needs to be free
From you and your insanity
But you are a family member
So he's forced to remember
But that shouldn't f'ing be
Michael deserves to be free

II

As cold as any day in December
You are his winter
You're no winner
Not the way I remember
And you never will be
Michael is a key
That unlocks the people's misery
I know your history
You are no mystery
What you're doing is hurting me
But that's a part of your story

But your being's not mandatory
I mean you can get wasted
I know you never tasted
Love like mine is too deep based
What you have said hasn't erased
The way I feel about him
Did you think I would doubt him?
Try to live without him
Simply because you talked about him
Yes I'm an angry fan
You try to screw my man
You should understand
You gon' see the back of my hand
I ain't never been hard on a ho
Until you came you know
I don't want Michael to know
But I would like to see you go
You know you're his kin
Ans that to him would be a sin
But that ain't what I'm in
I play the game to win
Malcolm said by whatever means necessary
You're too contrary
'Cause really though ordinarily
I wouldn't give you the time of day but he
Believes in his family
While I see a snake where a snake be
Just cause your tail is curled don't mean you're a key
You can't unlock this mystery
I told you Michael is the key
He's the man for me
Little girl you better see
If he don't protect you then you got to deal with me

III

Just a side note
In case you wanna vote
A political quote
The papers never wrote
But I heard it said so
When Clinton said oh
About Miss Harden
In the ice garden
His lips were moving
He said innocent until proven
But in Michael's case
He showed no face
I call that tasteless
His comments were baseless
Yet and still that's politics
The same old dirty tricks
And year after year
That's the way it's played here
Now back to the groove
When you made your move
Decided to accuse
Rhythm and blues
White socks and black shoes
It made international news
It started to confuse
People yet to choose
Who themselves will lose
If they're easy to amuse
But if we lose this icon
Put down because he trusted someone
Someone on the home run
A sister with a hidden gun
That is piling on the dirt
You know its gon' hurt

As bad as Captain Kirk
Being seen in Scottie's skirt
Michael trusted you
And loved you too
What are you gon' do
I need a hero too
And Michael will do
Anybody but you
Is it so hard to be true?
Leave that guy you're married to
That's what you should do
You don't love him so be honest and true
To the way Katherine and Joe raised you
But if you keep doing taboo
Then only God can save you

IV

There are people out there
That just don't care
You should stay clear
They're going nowhere
Understand me now girl
We live in a world
Dominated by evil girl
And that's the world
That will say we need you sister
Treat you like a magic crystal
But they want to form that blister
Want you to give them the pistol
So they can shoot him down in front of you
They won't say boo
But they will turn and they'll shoot you too
And it will be true
When Michael's through
They'll come after you

You must be a fool
Go back to school
Learn to keep your cool
Stop being their fool
You're no exception to the rule
You're on their schedule
Because you're playing their fool
That isn't back to school
That's pre-freedom school
I know you grew up like you were white
You grew up with Michael right
But you have threatened the good knight
He's in a great fight
He's in trouble right
Who are you if you help enemies in this fight?
What will you sacrifice to save this knight?
All devils can fight
And they got that appetite
Ask your mama and if I'm right
You come home to the light
They have the right of might
Being black here has never been easy
I'm not asking you to please me
But bitch don't tease me
The world isn't disease free
Michael earned his glory
Now you come along with this foul story
Like you know me—you don't know me
And you don't know how bad you look on TV
Michael is our hope and our God sent key

Chorus

Come home—you don't have to stay in Rome
We will send her to the psycho zone
This is the place you were born—come home
This is the place you were born—come home

I'll see your sister stops her wrong
What good am I if I'm not at least that strong?
I'll see your sister stops her wrong
What good am I if I'm not at least that strong?

The End

Joe Would Raise Hell

02/20/94

I

Any of 'em could've told you how it felt
They all knew Joe's belt
And when it was dealt
Your skin would melt
There was much work
Joseph was not a jerk
I haven't misread
He used his head
His toughness led
His children away from the dead
Streets of nowhere
And gave them a successful career
Michael my dear
Unlike some your father was there
It took a strong man
And a strong hand
His strength in command
Directed the band
And brought it to the Promised Land
Joe was that man
Not a perfect man
Not a holy but a strict man
Tell me if you can
What would have become of the band
The band without Joe?
There would've been no Jackson 5 show
He is the reason for that glow
It wouldn't have happened without Joe

Barry Gordy said so
So I respect him yo!
The one thing I know
Is that we need fathers to stay like Joe

II

Child abuse to tell the truth
Maybe for some youth
With parents strung out on the juice
Drugs can be a noose
Violence in the street
Violence in the beat
Are signs of a massive retreat
We're facing defeat
Where are you Joe?
Come back to the show
We need fatherhood to grow
The police would be saying no
Crack was found
Kids wouldn't be messing around
If a kid was Joe's son
He wouldn't have a gun
He wouldn't go on a drive by run
He wouldn't shoot anyone
You see under this sun
Things aren't always fun
But you could go to school
Without somebody acting a fool
Breaking the most important rule
Thinking being armed is cool
Nowadays kids can't learn
And can't 'til men like Joe return
Until then its burn baby burn
Joe made sure they learned
There were fortunes to be earned

A good investment will yield a good return
But with an A K forty seven
You're fourteen and on you way to Heaven
Or for trying to rob a Seven Eleven
You're in jail with life plus seven
But that wouldn't be so
If more fathers were like Joe

III

What about it Jermaine
You got the big brain
What's there to explain?
Joe had to maintain
You don't play with Katherine
And don't dog her children
Like Katherine the Great
Her involvement had weight
Some things you don't rehearse
She was as neat as a nurse
But she was a mother first
She saw her children star burst
This extraordinary woman
Who God sent an omen
Was unusually strong
Used her faith to hold on
But Joe wasn't gon' let 'em go wrong
Yet every time Joe phoned
He found her at home
Like Caesar in Rome
Her influence was strong
She could do no wrong
In Michael's young eyes
And so she was idolized
She didn't have paradise
But she's why he's so nice

And in her great silence
She controlled family violence
Because from time to time
When someone got out of line
Joe wasn't understanding or kind
Joe was all bizness mind

IV

The world is cruel
We're killing for fuel
Why not for black renewal
Save our black jewel
By any means necessary
I'm not contrary
Michael is legendary
And Joe's extraordinary
Guidance caused them
To become an American hymn
I thank God for him
And for all of them
God what a family
Joe didn't command me
So understand me
I love this family
Michael and Janet
Both rule the planet
Those who have dropped out
Haven't copped out
They're in the bizness
Can I get a witness?
A witness that poor blacks
Over poverty tracks
Gave us the Jackson Five
And though they had difficult lives
They did survive

'Cause Joe didn't jive
Look at the enterprise
That he helped realize
You can say what you want to say yo!
But in front of me don't disrespect Joe

Bridge

Kids wouldn't be going to jail
Instead they would excel
'Cause Joe would raise hell
Whip somebody's tail
'Cause Joe would raise hell
Whip somebody's tail
Kids wouldn't be going to jail
Instead they would excel
'Cause Joe would raise hell
Whip somebody's tail
'Cause Joe would raise hell
Whip somebody's tail
Kids wouldn't be going to jail
Instead they would excel

The End

Tell Him to Pay Them off Joe

Undated

I

After seeing part two
Of the Jackson family I knew
What Joe put them through
It was hard but true
Because of him they grew
Joe, look at what's happened to you
But I guessed what the boys would do
After the flack Joe they took off you
You should've known it too
But you didn't have a clue
Until they made you boohoo
Suddenly the big dog was through
The breakdown back to you
I said ah boohoo ooh boohoo
I guess they were really sore
They didn't want your guidance anymore
Though you had helped with every score
And opened every door
But you put yourself ashore
And they didn't want you anymore
Joe you had been cruel for years
And though I felt your tears
Through the applause and the cheers
Joe, they were facing new frontiers
Then suddenly Michael broke away
And suddenly there was no more to say
After you did Katy that way
I knew things wouldn't stay

The same old Joseph way
When you hurt and betray
It comes back one day
So Joe what can I say
It was your time to pay
When you hurt her you hurt MJ
And you can't hurt the king
Joe you did a foolish thing
Not even you can hurt the king
Not as long as he wants to sing
Not as long as he wants to swing
Not as long as he does his thing
Not as long as he wears the ring

II

And of all people Joe
You should know
Katherine's woe
Is Michael's so
You were lucky again
She let you stay in
Her love did not end
You did something bad my friend
Her forgiveness is noble Joe
She could've let you go
But being a queen she said no
Michael I still love Joe
And the rest of the story you know
So you must know
You've been lucky Joe
To have a woman who honored you so
You have the greatest kids in the world
Except for that one little girl
Not a diamond but a flawed pearl
The one thing that's certain is she's your girl

I was just thinking and looking back
On how hard it was to be black
Thinking over every recent attack
What we have and what we lack
Look at the crazy things you did
God knows how you kept it hid
And this thing with Michael and that kid
Isn't it awful what they say he did?
But I saw how strong Katherine's morals were
Too strong for something like this to occur
Looking at you both I know that Michael is no sneaky
    little fox
Because he was raised by her and an ox
I hope you taught him how to box
So he can fight back after detox
There are a lot of whites on prescription fixes
And all kinds of legitimate mixes
But we hardly hear about their in-betwixt(s)
It's hard to win against triple sixes
And in all the things you hear
You hear how bad black is this year
I'm just glad Michael never broke
For smack or that coke
I know you will help him cope
Help him climb back up the rope
At least I want the world to know I hope
This destruction is not in his horoscope

III

Joe I'm no psychic expert
But after I saw his Bucharest concert
I knew he wasn't Captain Kirk
But good things for him do work
Sooner or later something had to come
He had too much money to have freedom

He has always been so giving
And when living the life he was living
There was gonna be a shark
Swimming around in the dark
Somebody who wouldn't pass on an opportunity
That would attack without impunity
It wasn't like that in the old community
Now Michael has little or no immunity
Because his heart is trusting and kind
Even with a highly developed mind
To some things he is blind
If you had been there he wouldn't be in this bind
But he had to grow up and go out on his own
He had to learn how to handle the unknown
And you taught him well
But Joe this thing could be hell
Michael is a black male
Caught up in the worse kind of fairy tale
Did you know Peter Pan was a girl?
Does that rock your world?
You've got to work something out Joe
After all you're the old pro
This child can be a terrible foe
He could cause Michael a lot of woe
I don't have to tell you about the tabloid press
And what they manifest
And how they're shaping things in the west
If his lawyers ain't the best
This thing could turn into a mess
Not to mention a criminal arrest
Even if he wins the court room scene
He may still be viewed as a subhuman being

Chorus

Tell him to pay them off Joe
Tell him to pay them off Joe
Tell him to pay them off Joe
The only way to end this show
Is to pay them off Joe
Tell him to pay them off Joe

The End

Mrs. Katherine

03/18/94

Like Michael the subpoenaing of his mother outraged me. I too could not see what useful purpose it served. It seemed like harassment to me. In a situation of the dollars against indictment, perhaps he's the first black ever to obtain the kind of wealth and the world fame he has, and that's what I think this thing is really about. If he wasn't who he was—he wouldn't be pre-tried by the press, and he would have a chance to a fair trial.

I

Mrs. Katherine: take the stand
Do you know the man?
The man from Neverland
The second Peter Pan
Who is still making a kill
Is he that for real?
Will he accept a D.A. deal?
Does he have the will?
The entertainment skill
Tell us about the way you feel
When you see him do you kneel?
Now what did he wanna be?
Let's say at the age of three?
Has he ever been carefree?
Or is he really what you see?
Is he afraid of the grand jury?
Feels like he's from Missouri

You know show me
Show me that you know me
When did he first sing?
Was he smart in everything?
When did he start wanting to be a king?
Is his thing a natural swing?
And what about all that love
He's got—did he get that from above?
Before push comes to shove
Where is the other glove?
Being mistreated why does he still love?
Why doesn't he feel like a wounded dove?
Why are they treating him like a crow?
Why they are doing that I don't know
But people wanna know—you know
You're his mother they'll believe whatever you say so

II

Shouldn't he hate those
Who down Negroes?
And tell us what goes
Goes about the nose?
Why is there no hatred in his prose?
Where did he get those clothes?
His fans love him so
Don't or do they know
Even after the surgery he's still a Negro?
Some don't want him to be a hero
You know cause he came from zero
He started there years ago
And he's been a good Negro
But they don't want a Negro superhero
Playing Captain Nemo
Did he look like you
Way back when he was two?

When he started talking
Was he also moonwalking?
Do you remember the time
When he first heard rhythm and rhyme?
If you do what was his very first line?
He's so good is he a natural find
Or something Joe designed?
And are you as a mother blind
To what might be a crime?
Do you remember the time
Before he reached his prime
"The King of Pop time?"
Were there early signs that he was gay?
Did you know he'd change night to day?
And if he's like they say?
Will he live the gay way?

III

We know all women
And some fans who are men
Want to know about Ben
His childhood friend
Is it true Ben had hair
All over him everywhere?
And did your son care
About Ben living under the frizgadaire?
We know he's very humane
But was having such a friendship sane
And can you explain
The problem he had with Jermaine?
Why and how is that?
Ben was just a rat
Why didn't the family have a cat?
It's said that Michael sat
Night after night with Ben

Is it true that back then
He was comfortable with Ben
Because he had no other friend
Why didn't he have a dog?
Why didn't he have a pet frog?
Or pet pig or hog?
When he talked to Ben was there a dialog?
Since it's said a dog is man's best friend
Why did he choose Ben?
Do you remember when
He first told you about Ben?
Or is Ben a part of some myth
That no one wants to deal with?
He loves animals but he's no blacksmith
Do you wanna answer or take the fifth?

IV

Lady Katherine if you please
Was he ever a little tease?
Did he often lose his keys?
Did he ever scrape his knees?
Was he always a nice boy?
Was he always the real McCoy?
What was his favorite toy?
Did he share his things as a boy?
Did he like girls back then?
Let's say around ten
Did he have a girlfriend
Or was it all-pretend?
Why isn't he like the others
Like his other brothers?
They seem to have had their lovers
Did their time with them under covers
How long was it known
That he had outgrown

The group before he left?
Does he write what he sings himself
Or does it come from someone else?
Why didn't he protect himself?
Is he what he seems?
Is he disturbed by dreams?
Were his nightmares real?
Were they reasons for the pill?
What's the real deal?
What to him is real?
How does he differ from the others?
Does he get alone with his brothers?

V

Lady Katherine if you don't mind
Do you believe Justice is blind?
Do you think you might find
Life in America to blacks is unkind?
Aren't blacks serving more time
Or do you believe on up the line
Being rich and black will be a crime?
Under such an apartheid system
Will your son be a victim?
Should whites be encouraged to go
And compete against the Negro
When all we have is the show?
Why are they disrupting his flow?
Why are they dropping this bomb?
Don't they know Blacks are not dumb?
That Blacks recognize your son
For all the good he has done
In the name of fun
He is Number One
While others have used the gun
But not your son

He has never used a weapon
He has never hurt anyone
Yet his kingdom is here
His wisdom is clear
He's a multimillionaire
But there is real danger in this smear
Does he send roses on Mother's Day?
Isn't he always personal that way?
Is he straight or is he gay?
Does he have anybody other than Liz in LA?

VI

Does he buy you special things
Bracelets and diamond earrings?
How long has he wanted to be the Pan?
Who helped him design Neverland?
Why do they love him so much in Japan?
Do you think they understand
The charges that he may face?
Why is the Japanese race
Unconcerned over what's being called a disgrace?
Does he hate his own race?
Are things all right between him and Joe?
Does Joe think he's gay or do you know?
Why didn't he sing at the Jackson Family Honor's Show?
Has Latoya always been that slow?
Back to Vegas then
Was it all a pretend
To thank a personal friend?
Why did Janet not stay to the end?
Do you think he'll find
In this country that justice is blind?
Will the courts be kind?
Is it too much to risk this time?
If he's found guilty of a crime

Where would you like him to do his time?
Shouldn't he be treated like any other Negro
Who may or may not have an eagle to show?
Should we block his flow?
Why should we treat him like a hero?
Can he after this still dominate the stage?
Could he usher in a new age?
Aren't you afraid of the rage?
Will he look good in prison beige?

Chorus

Mrs. Katherine, a mother has a right to protect her child
A mother has a right to protect her child
Mrs. Katherine, a mother has a right to protect her child
A mother has a right to protect her child

The End

Lady Katy

Undated

I

She's a kind and sensitive lady
She believes in nothing shady
And everybody calls her Katy
Her belief in God does not come lately
She's believed all her life and she believes greatly
She's proud of every baby
She says God gave me
She says I owe it all to him because he made me
She has raised her children well
None should go to Hell
It's a success story any mother would be proud to tell
One is the world's most popular male
Though her family is great it has not been an easy life
There has been a great deal of strife
After all she is Joseph's wife
Sometimes that cuts like a knife
But she's been true and faithful from the start
She gave Michael his big heart
Her depth of soul is in his art
It's the reasons he hasn't been torn apart
They all owe her a great deal
She has been silent and she has kept still
Allowing each one to develop their skill
But through it all she's been real
Cooking and cleaning she gave them love
You can see it all in the "One Glove"
They said she'd never push or shove
Instead she offers kindness and love

Michael credits her with giving him so much
She's the reason behind his gentle touch
Though he continues to search
When he's home she takes him to church

II

You're running straight talk when you should be Ice Tea-
    ing
You lock up your heart but your emotions are still fleeing
You're out here looking but you're not seeing
This is what it takes for a woman to be a special human
    being
Katy grew up with nothing at all
If she stumbled she didn't have far to fall
Yet this woman stood very tall
Not in height cause that was small
With one leg shorter than the other
She met and married this brother
Joseph Jackson was that lover
From their union the world would discover
For from them great children would be born
Though the greatest would suffer scorn
He would be battered and worn
And treated like a 'child of the corn'
It was by God's grace and under his divine protection
That she raised her children and gave them direction
Darwin said it's a matter of natural selection
Though I doubt she ever saw that reflection
She raised them with God at the top
The music they made would never stop
God knows she had a good crop
One would become the King of Pop
They had only love when they started out
It was a hard life and they were filled with doubt
But believing in God they took the harder route

And that belief and hard work brought them a turnabout
Katy never failed her children and God never failed her
She saw him through every blur
And grace and mercy did occur
One day the world would know them because of her

III

For a poor black woman her morals were strong
She never cheated though often left alone
She never did her husband wrong
Her children grew up and they were gone
Most of them before they were grown
It must have been hard in that big house alone
But she understood how you make a song
Knowing one day they would be worldwide known
Because of the dignity and strength she had shown
Her children went out and made it on their own
Michael setting highest on the throne
With the kind of power that makes you feel alone
But like his mother he has been strong
The winds may blow hard and they may blow long
But as he remembers her he will remember her song
A song that says God is great and you must hold on
Be patient with him for you are not alone
Even when things are very wrong
And you're beaten down, beat up and feeling worn
Ride to the end of day for a new day will be born
Stand in the sunshine and think of his love
The birds of prey come but so does the dove
For as sure as God is in heaven above
Mothers do not abandon the children they love
Remember on those cold rainy days the way she raised
    you
God will send the sun and you can say Lord we praise you
We knew you would because everything obeys you

Katy is a good woman and her goodness shines through
When you were sick or hungry she took care of you
She did what all-good mothers do
She believes in God and from her view
He has taken care of her and he will take care of you

Chorus

She's the mother of the king—y'all sing: Lady Katy –
    Lady Katy
She's the mother of the king—now sing Lady Katy –
    Lady Katy
You know it's good when the music is charged up –
    charged up
I knew that he would because his music is charged up –
    charged up
She's the mother of the king—y'all sing: Lady Katy –
    Lady Katy
She's the mother of the king—now sing Lady Katy –
    Lady Katy
You know it's good when the music is charged up –
    charged up
I knew that he would because his music is charged up –
    charged up

The End

You're Not Gon' Stop His Flow

Undated

I

If Michael is on top you're under
So you bust out wit' this plunder
Damn it's no wonder
You're afraid because he makes thunder
So you start messing wit' his mama
Damn that's another bummer
Give it to me drummer
Do you need this trauma?
Is that gon' make you somebody I don't know
What do you think about it Negro?
Lost your brain sliding in that snow
I remember when you wore an Afro
Under your cop hat
And we're proud to do that
But now you're jealous of Michael's act
Jealous of his impact
You bust out here now looking for something
In the clubs we're still jumping
Michael started something
Everybody in here bumping
Like they're having a fit
That you boys can't git
Every time he releases it's a hit
I don't wanna hear that bullshit
Why you wanna bring the lady down
You're always f-ing around
You MF-ing clown
You ought to be at the dog pound

All you're doing is blowing this town
While Michael is steady getting down
Don't come here messing around
No one is gon' break down
You might as well leave his mama alone
Messing wit' her ain't gon' get you known
But it can get you gone
Dead and buried in the graveyard alone

II

Another episode in this melodrama
Ain't got no gun but I got some lumber
Don't mess wit' his mama
You hear me plumber?
Out here running pipe
For spite and media hype
Talking about he's the type
You want another stripe
Is that gon' help you get up the force
To continue all this pain and remorse
I think I know this course
I want you to take me to the source
That guy behind that door
Isn't he the one you're working for?
A fool like you can't setup a chore
That you don't know how to score
If I could line you up in my site
I could make everything all right
Bang-bang down goes your spite
You'll be dead and buried by tomorrow night
I'm not threatening you
I'm just letting you
Know what I might do
If he asks me to
I'll have to put some hurt on you

The kind of hurt you never knew
You'll wish you had withdrew
But you won't cause the Devil's in you
I told you not to mess wit' Lady Katy
Dick Tracy is Warren Baity
Punk you should be out there chasing Sadie
After all she's better than your old lady
You come to work frustrated
People moving up and you hate it
Michael's up there and you want him castrated
Can't understand why you didn't and he made it

III

Before I get to you take a number
How would you feel if it were your mama
UMF I don't need this drama
You gon' look up and see a stealth bomber
Getting ready to unload on you
And there will be nothing you can do
Except eat your do-do
It will be over for you
You won't even see it coming
Until it starts bombing
What you're doing is alarming
Someday somebody gon' be farming
With or over your body punk
Whether you end up in a trunk
Or in some alley an old worn out drunk
Nothing can stop the funk
Not you, not the DA or city hall
All y'all gon' fall
Just 'cause a man stands tall
Y'all gon' make him crawl
Go on make your call
Michael will not play ball

Know what I'm saying screw y'all
Go head hook up your U-haul
Take everything in his house if you want to
Null of that shit gon' help you
But a fool got to do what a fool got to do
But after you're through he should sue you
Take from you what you tried to take from him
They will replace you wit' another one of them
You're not Johnny Weissmuller so you can't be Jungle Jim
But you got to steal from a black don't you Slim?
You got to stand in that review
You want all big shot eyes on you
You wanna do this—do what you got to do
Go after his mama he's not gon' roll over for you

Chorus

I don't give a damn what you know
You're not gon' stop his flow
I don't give a damn I'm telling you so
You're not gon' cop his flow
Cops sitting around drinking coca colas
Assholes sitting around filling quotas
I don't give a damn what you know
You're not gon' stop his flow

The End

Thank You Jermaine

03/23/94

I

I have watched you on TV
Pleading with her for me
And other fans I must say Jermaine
I fear it was in vain
If she was called by the grand jury
Get caught up in all the media fury
In all that drudgery
She'll commit perjury
Her fear will make her lie
Fear of losing the TV eye
We know that she's ill
Nevertheless they will
Like a pusher to a junky
Use her like a trained monkey
Until they have the dirt
They need to make it hurt
That's what they will do
May God protect you?
You seem to be to me
Willing to do much so he
Won't be injured by his family
I'm only a servant really
And that's all I can be
To the glory of his majesty
In his anointed reign
He is in all things my king
What else in spirit do we own?
All other powers are unknown

I then cherish his throne
My pledge is to keep it strong

II

I realize the family in this
Has suffered from her Judas kiss
Thrown into this dark abyss
I wonder will I miss
Approaching dead ahead
Our minds slowly growing dead
And we are so misled
Going from the black into red
For months now I've shook
Inside the pages of this book
Where I am I dare not look
I fear that this little Captain Hook
Has sworn an oath to the dark prince
So I make no pretense
I will serve in Michael's defense
And do what he designates from hints
I ask you oh faithful brother
Tell him even if they double
And bubble this trouble
I will serve no other
I aim to stay a knight of his court
Until evil shall abort
Give up this brutal effort
I'll struggle against this vile report
The wild dogs track him now
Hoping so much for a fallen cow
A quick kill would please them now
But I know God will stay them off somehow
We are prepared to take this hit
With all my will I'll try to use it
To drive the beast back into the pit
Only death shall make me quit

III

I am your brother by skin
And by the situation we're in
My blood is thick not thin
The hair on my head and chin
Carries the same distinction
I will fight this extinction
He's in my deepest thought
The battle will be fought
The lesson will be taught
The precious rain caught
How I wish I could be there
To tell him how much I care
To take away his pain at least my share
Oh to be once in life in his sphere
These are the things I dream
That God will indeed redeem
His honor from those seeking extreme
They don't want him to be supreme
But his is a great gift that must be kept
So I pledge all I can do to help
I've put every single dance step
To memory—I have not slept
It seems for so very long
Thinking about his every song
Wondering my God how long
Can evil be so high up and strong
Please tell him for me Jermaine
Some of us do share his pain
And we're fighting this attempt to destroy
A person who has given us joy
They have made him a decoy
But he's still the one we most enjoy

IV

He must be troubled by what's said
Tell him he need not be afraid
His armies stand ready to raid
And we will not fade
Whether he owes society or not
We're passed getting hot
Tired of him being on the spot
Look at what the Harden girl got
They talk as if justice is for all
Only a fool would play ball
Some say why praise him so
As if they raised him so
Watch him from a child grow
He was our leader from the word go
The way he moved across the floor
We're not gon' let them close this door
We're not gon' let them make this score
We can't take it anymore
In spirit I've been at every show
He has ever done so you know
I will stand behind him
We will not let evil undermine him
They just want to bind him
Like Samson then blind him
But unlike Samson
We will pay his ransom
In our hearts he will always be our handsome
Prince—though they depict him as a Manson
We do not accept their lies
The truth is in his eyes
And all we need realize
Is that we will never compromise

Chorus

Thank you Jermaine
For being there again and again
Thank you Jermaine
For the injury you must sustain
Thank you Jermaine
For standing by our king Jermaine
Thank you Jermaine
For being there again and again

The End

And Joe I'm A Lot Like You and You're A Lot Like Me

Undated

I

The Jacksons are an American Dream
After seeing the movie again things seem
That Joe you were mighty mean
And not much else in between
Nevertheless the credit is yours
Because you open the doors
Wrote the musical scores
And though my heart pours
For what's happened with compassion
I admit I myself in a like fashion
Punished for every wrong action
In the end I got no satisfaction
Luckily I saw the hurt and did a turn about
But seeing this story I doubt
If you ever found that out
But I saw them dance and shout
I saw them power their way
From the ghetto across the USA
Then as the world gave them play
It fell in love with them — especially MJ
For ten years night and day
They were on the minds of every deejay
Hit after hit their orbit didn't decay
Until they broke up and faded away
But that was in the wake of a superstar
The brightest ever so far
If I could see Michael I would say Michael you are

And it all started over Tito playing your guitar
Playing it in secret for over a year
Because of the fear
That you would not share
But I think now they know you care

II

Sometimes it hard to show our family we care
And that we really want to share
Ourselves more openly but we drown in our fear
Even though it's often not clear
It's a wonder they obey us never seeing our love
Just the push and the shove
You were a crippled dove
Afraid to land so you circled above
Out of the reach of entanglement
You bought the school books, food and paid the rent
You went in debt and spent
To secure their future in entertainment
You worked their little fingers to the bone
And you always kept them close at home
Maybe this growing up all alone
Created at least in Michael a no escape syndrome
A thing that he has never outgrown
But his love for his mother is strong
Even if what he feels for you is somewhat unknown
I know he will address this wrong
And for her and his fans he will comeback strong
You might have kept them alone
But she gave them something that has grown
And she is the one who influences the throne
Sometimes a man can hold on too tight
And though what he wants is right
His continuity is destroyed in the fight
By the unpleasantness of his encrypted appetite

Therefore he's driven from the light
That he himself helped to ignite
Such it seems has been your plight
Because fright is always followed by flight

III

And though you made them universal
And certainly you make them commercial
And here of late one of them controversial
Every moment with you was in rehearsal
They never celebrated Christmas or holidays
Because those are not Jehovah ways
Still in all of this craze
Looking at my own crazy days
I too looked through a one-way glaze
And though I give you praise
There were other ways
A less restrictive phase
I know because I've seen those rays
I've had my own children to raise
I didn't believe in holidays
But having lost so much I changed my ways
And as imperfect as I may be
These things luckily I did see
They were happening to me
I was depriving my family
Now Christmas celebrations are mandatory
Yet I agree the way we do the story
Such pagan practices are hardly holy
We lie to our children because it's Christmasee
We tell them about flying reindeers
Who transverse the sky as though by musical chairs
Carrying a little fat man who cares
But more important than that we tell them that day is
    theirs

And that's a lie—so you see Joe there's a lot of you in me
And there's also the possibility
That because of this philosophy
We have caused our families unnecessary misery

Chorus

And Joe I'm a lot like you and you're a lot like me
We both have had an adoring loving family
And Joe like you I have caused them misery
And Joe like you I was trying to escape poverty
And Joe like you the same things happened to me
And Joe like you I wanted them to be free
And Joe like you I tried to do that financially
And Joe like you they have been lucky for me
And Joe like you we have been blessed physically
And Joe like you I know this literally
And Joe like you I hope to improve spiritually
And Joe I'm a lot like you and you're a lot like me

The End

As Long As You Are Strong

Revised 06/23/96

I

She said of Michael's childhood
It was mostly good
He hardly ever misunderstood
Like the others would
Even as a child
He always had style
A professional smile
He never ran wild
Joe kept a close eye on them all
He was determine they would not fall
And though they didn't play ball
They answered a greater call
They were gold record prospectors
They had no protectors
No boyhood correctors
But they found the ground connectors
Under Barry's leadership
On that Motown trip
And Joe was so hipped
That none slipped
Or fell along the way
He knew that stardom someday
Would come their way
And so did Michael J.
Even way back then
Signs said that he would be a man among men
Not yet himself ten
Later he'd long for the child he had never been

But no one sees pass the sunset
And the moonlight that we get
If impatient one may bitterly regret
Getting caught in a self nourishing fantasy net
A child plays in every man's mind
And if that play time
Is unwillingly left behind
Ugly vines can climb
Into the secret world of that girl or boy
It may harbor monsters that can destroy
The simplest human joy
On that unsafe convoy
We roll through our restless days
Seeking only what we crave
A man can be rich but still a slave
If trapped by unchanging ways
And though Michael fulfilled his future glaze
He never gave up his "wanna be a child" ways
Undoubtedly this preference
This desire for adolescence
Almost destroy his essence
Left him with a tarnished reference

II

As Five Stair-steps they started out
A vision that only they dreamed about
But even then they turned it out
And soon there was little doubt
That the world would know
These kids who presented at the Apollo
Singing and dancing and stole the show
At Motown their talents would overflow
Michael in the movie said to Barry Gordy
I wish you were my daddy
He was impressed with Mr. Gordy

But thank God Joe was his daddy
Because Joe gave him genes
The things that make human beings
Into record selling machines
That put them on the television screens
Of an American Bandstand
The boys would land
And taking command
They reached the promise land
If it means anything to be in the top ten
Michael was destined way back then
In the group he was the kingpin
You could see his great talent within
There is no question about their success
As a sold out group in the west
But Joe wanted victory in every contest
In the world he wanted them to be the best
But success has its price
Though Michael is nice
Inside we all have some ice
We all fall short of Paradise
So it was difficult to accept
That they no longer needed their father's help
It was a risky step
All those years together they had been kept
They were finally breaking up
There would be no making up
Though they tried reshaping up
Inside Michael a whole new thing was waking up
And like Diana years befo'e
Time came for him to go
He had to leave the J-5 show
He had to go solo
His first superstar call
Came with "Off The Wall"
For awhile it looked as if he would fall
But then Thriller came and out did them all

It was the mountain he had topped
I knew then, he couldn't be stopped

III

No one person has ever done
Or had such an impressive run
Or walk more tall and won
No one but Katherine's son
In records sales everywhere
Suddenly he was out there
Claiming more than a king's share
Showing the world he did care
About every single aspect
Of each and every project
He labored to make perfect
I call that the Joe Jackson effect
Because perfection was Joseph's thing
And Michael who we call king
Learned from Joe how to do everything
To do it like it was done by a king
The father influenced the son
And that's the way it should be done
So again I thank you Mr. Jackson
Because your will has been done
Because Michael is your son
In whom you hit a home run
But Katherine according to your son
You were the most influential one
In giving him his depth of heart
Katherine you played a significant part
In the development of Michael and his art
It was he who said my mother's very smart
An unnamed queen from the start
A queen of courage and heart
Who always stressed decency

A thing that has been called recently
In question about the king
It is no less an ugly thing
For a man who has never been a child
To be accused of thing so wild
It is strange and unnatural
I believe it is the financial
Weaving of a web to destroy
Not his but our hope and joy
For he has become more than songs to enjoy
So I question the story about the boy
How much of it is fantasy
We will never know—it was an act of mercy
That Michael rose from ghetto misery
To claim a place in world history
Unlike any entertainer before
Michael has opened the door
As if Heaven wrote the score
We stand now upon that brave shore

Bridge

I'm here for you as long as you are strong
And I swear I will help you carry on
We will fight evil until evil is gone
We won't give up the throne
I'm here for you as long as you are strong
And I swear I will help you carry on

The End

The Exhortation

Seeing the Jackson's Family Honors show, like many fans, I wanted Michael to perform. But when he didn't I understood. I still felt in the future he could make a real difference because of his great popularity among all people, and his ability to influence a world market, he was in position to do things that few of my people dream of doing. His incredible talent, charm, sophistication, dedication and discipline had lifted him up and placed him in the eyes of the world. He might not have chose politics, but his enormous wealth; world leadership position and the style and content of his ballads had destined him to be such a figure. We desperately needed a victor, I had for some time thought of him as that person. Suddenly it wasn't make believe anymore. He was already doing great things and when I think of how much higher he could lift the Negro banner, I am amazed. His survival was precedent now and I didn't know how I could help but I dedicated all my efforts to completing this task. He had been damaged from the attacks and I felt that I had to keep lifting him up. Lifting him until he himself realized that they couldn't destroy him for to do that they would have to destroy all of us.

You have to ask yourself do fans love Michael or his music? The answer is we love both. True fans find it hard separating the two. Michael is his music and the music is Michael but there's so much more to him than simply being a performing artist. He gives to charities all the time. He really wants to save the world for our children but can he, can we, can anybody? Can anybody save us from us?

All Rise For the King

02/22/94

I

Faced with attack
If you look back
Who loves your art
Fans of your heart
We'll be with you
And we'll be true
What can we do
When we love you
We won't let them
Push you off of a limb
You are our hymn
Our precious gem
We're down for that
You are so top hat
And the top act
Just one more fact
Come back to the stage
Live out your age
Use your great gift
To give our hearts a lift
You're like a Duke of Earl
You could have any girl
Nothing can stop you in this world
The truth to us has been unfurled
And because you're a black seed
We want you to succeed
Carry out the blessed deed
Give us back what we need

Oh my precious king
You're everything
That our hearts sing
You make us swing
And for the gift you bring
We've made you king
It doesn't matter how strange
They try to arrange
What you are to us
You'll always have our trust
And our devotion
I say with great emotion
There will be no erosion
Of your explosion
Because you comfort the pain
We need you again and again
May your reign never end
You are a friend
To countless many
You're worth every penny
To those who see you perform
In that electric storm
Where hearts become sworn
Your kingdom was born

II

There is only one you
In the world who
We are loyal to
And we love you
You say you love us too
There's nothing for you
We would not do
We would do anything for you
Including follow you

Through hell if we have too
We know you're true
The kingdom belongs to you
You are the throne
You have no clone
Only you turn us on
And in that zone
All wrong is gone
But if you leave we will be alone
We'll grow in sadness and mourn
For to you we are sworn
On the day you were born
Gabriel must've blew his horn
Our gain was heaven's loss
And we will pay whatever the cost
To save ourselves from your loss
We will carry your cross
Evil has come here hoping to slay
You my king today
Your greatness it wants to lay
Down but the sun is out today
We will drive evil away
We will have our say
You're like a wind
Blowing from within
Over our despair
You blow so fair
From here to the Red Square
Even there they care
They hear your words
They flock to you like birds
They stampede like herds
Becoming Michael nerds
They follow you everywhere
Like you they also care
And they want to share
With people everywhere

Yes your sound is loud and clear
You relieve the fear
And so they cheer
Because you give them atmosphere

III

So why suffer grotesque
Statements if you request
In one great protest
We'll destroy the tabloid Press
Put fevered minds to rest
If that's what you address
Your fans to manifest
We'll destroy their ugliness
The talk shows too no less
They'll not disturb your rest
I know you're hurting too
Some are afraid of you
Because you are unique
Sculptured from the finest teak
It is your time to peak
War can be won by technique
So fight them with every song
That way you can't go wrong
No one is as strong
As you are with a song
If for the cause of freedom I die
Then no greater cause have I
Than to sound the battle cry
And to lift the banners high
Let them try to bring you down
All they want is your crown
I am not their painted clown
Though I wear my face in a frown
I wear it for you my king

'Cause to your fans you're everything
We want to hear you sing
We want to see you swing
We want you to do what you do
And because we love you
We won't let them break through
We will give our all for you
Protect you from the dark
And the evil news shark
The wild dogs in TV Park
You can make your mark
Upon our passion
It will be whatever you fashion
You are the main attraction
The man of action
The driven passion
You give us complete satisfaction

IV

Your enemies come and they rage
They want to destroy your age
But your fans on and off stage
Are writing down every page
Though time won't stand still
Believe me we are for real
We know it's a money deal
You say it's wrong to hurt and kill
That's why they want you down
They want to drive you underground
After you're gon' destroy your sound
Those things promoted by the crown
How can they understand?
Like any other fan
I am willing to stand
For the man from Neverland

And there are many like me
We believe in his majesty
What else could he be?
He is setting us free
He is on the pages in this book
He is where so many look
We won't allow him to be took
Not by Hook or crook
You see I really think
He is on the brink
Of establishing a worldwide link
That evil doers cannot sink
Though destruction may come
You must hold onto freedom
Hold onto your kingdom
Until Armageddon
Lift up your eyes
Together with us realize
Even with the best of desires
There will be fires
And those who despise
Transmit their lies
But this ugly untrue
Will not destroy you
Hear me my king
And return and sing
And do your thing
Make the world swing
Go back into the center ring
We love you my king
Come back to us again
And be our friend
With you we could spend
Eternity as free men

V

So trouble is deep
And trouble is steep
And you can't sleep
Because of a creep
That's in all of us
There's no one to trust
Brothers are down from a bust
Heaven did not want us
Because we're this way
Listen to what I say
An angel gave us away
In hell this very day
The truth is coming true
Darkness is after you
Spreading TV taboo
But you got to stand true
It can't stop your mission
You must get in condition
And force evil's remission
We'll be your partition
Your shield through the transition
Love has been a tradition
With you and it's everywhere
You go—even here
Where with a smear
Enemies create fear
They breathe badness on you
But that won't make us less true
Whatever you want we will do
We'll do that for you
So many of us shirk
Seeing evil at work
We fear and we irk
But we know your great work

To the world is a gift
A gift you were born with
You're not a myth
As you rise you lift
Us up and because of your great hope
We will be able to cope
On this dangerous slope
For you are hope
So sing us a song
And sing it long
And sing it strong
Sing it against all things wrong
The music is in you
It's cutting through
The darkness and it will redeem you
And with that save us too

Chorus

All rise for the king
All eyes on the king
All rise for the king
All eyes on the king
The king of pop and swing
The king of pop and swing
All rise for the king
All eyes on the king
He's the king of everything
That makes our hearts sing
All rise for the king
All eyes on the king
Michael is the king
The king of pop and swing

The End

I Hire And Fire Security

02/24/94

I

Listen, I decide
And I'm tired
I know what transpired
You're undesired
And you're fired
The king is to be admired
I will abide
If they decide
Not to roast your hide
Save your pride
If that's all you have inside
God grant you a safe ride
Security is first of course
We're trained to use force
We have to protect the source
And we will without remorse
Don't act like you've been robbed
You had a good job
You didn't have to be a slob
Get skiska barbed
All you had to do was work
But you sold out like a jerk
And like Captain Kirk
Traitors make me irk
I know the rule
I've been more than cool
But when an employee acts a fool
Get stubborn like a mule

Threatened the Supercool
I use my tool
I fire the fool
Watch him ride out on that mule
I got to do what the man says boy
He's the real McCoy
I'm in his employ
The job I do is my joy
I don't try to have it my way
Use scandal for a payday
I'm loyal to the man okay
I wouldn't have it any other way

II

When someone gives you a job
You honor that job
You don't sell out the news mob
All they wanna do is pillage and rob
They'll give you a buck or two
And then they'll screw you
That's the way they do you
What's up with you
Ain't nobody else gon' hire you
Ain't nobody else gon' try you
Once I fire you
No one else will hire you
Your references will say undesirable
Under that will be written unreliable
Do you think that will make you viable?
Even if it is survivable
You'll still be labeled a fool
You don't mess with the Supercool
That's the golden rule
He's number one in the world fool
Son this ain't no movie

And what you did was not groovy
Don't try to pull one on me
If they had asked me
I would have said it's all a lie
I would have been the man's alibi
He's why I have my piece of the pie
You put your own thumb in your eye
Eye pain will make you cry
All I can say son is good bye
I must admit life is hard
But I'm captain of the guard
And captain of this yard
Firing you is a reward
As I said I am captain of the guard
Pick up your check and get off my yard

III

Now look I hired you
And I've fired you
If they inspired you
Tell them I retired you
I can understand that you're young
And obviously dumb
But when you're among
The superstardom
You learn to see and not see
And boy that's reality
You should have consulted me
Before you went on TV
With that I'm a fool interview
And now nobody will hire you
They won't even try you
In Hollywood that's the way they do
So draw your half time
You've committed no crime

Except show your behind
You must've been out of your mind
And since this is the land of the earthquake
Let me give you something you can equate
Remember the guy who reported Watergate
After that he never got a break
He should have been a hero but instead
He might as well have had his rights read
Suddenly his career was dead
He's the boss and I'm living off of his 'bread
He didn't do nothing I said
But if that don't make you afraid
After that Watergate raid
The dude should have had it made
The boy should've got paid
And guarding was his trade
The way it is he got played
That means when you are a spade
You just try to stay in the game
You don't disrespect nobody with a name

Bridge

I hire security and I fire security
There is no annuity in security
Loyalty doesn't require purity
And you don't show ambiguity
Especially if you're in security
I hire security and I fire security

The End

Maybe You Don't Know

02/26/96

I

Maybe you don't know the world is coming to an end
Maybe you don't know that you are not my friend
Maybe you don't know that you are hurting me
But you'd better find out because I'm tired of it you see
Maybe you don't know wrong from right
Maybe you don't know day from night
Maybe you don't know the trouble for me—you invite
But you better find out because it's making me uptight

II

Maybe you don't know you can't have it both ways
Maybe you don't know that no one makes all the plays
Maybe you don't know anything but your evil ways
But you better find out because I'm in an anger phase
Maybe you don't know that your lies really hurt
Maybe you don't know how to get out of the dirt
Maybe you don't know that I'm not a little jerk
But you better find out because I'm going to work

III

Maybe you don't know about the right to privacy
Maybe you don't know about the fight inside me
Maybe you don't know and don't know how to stop
But you better find out and you better stop
Maybe you don't know that there's good and bad

Maybe you don't know how to subtract and add
Maybe you don't know that I'm a lot like my dad
But you better find out before I really get mad

Bridge

Maybe you don't know but I know you know
That you are making it a difficult show
Maybe you don't know that when I say no—I mean no
And you don't know you're blocking my window but I
    know
And that's a threat so I'm upset
It's a sure bet that I repay a debt
Maybe you don't know but I know everyone I owe
And I know just where they go after every show
And hey! Maybe it's you that you don't know but I know

The End

You got Me Down

02/26/94

I

Take night from day
Just take it away
I got nothing to say
You know the way
I'm feeling today
Since you went away
The debt I got to pay
The fool I got to play

II

Why did you leave?
Do you want me to believe
That you didn't deceive
So why did you leave?
No one will believe
That I'm easy to deceive
Why did you leave?
What should I believe?

III

I'm asking for emergency care
I've needed it for a year
Your voice is all I hear
In the papers your name is everywhere
Crushing what I hold dear

But I'll out last the smear
This darkness will clear
Though now loneliness is all I share

IV

I'm so rich I'm poor
I can't close the door
Until I know the score
Don't you love me anymore?
I got to know for sure
I guess I'm immature
I need so badly the cure
What can I do to keep love pure?

Bridge

I'm telling my friends
And telling my fans
Telling my friends
And telling my fans
That you got me down
Almost on the ground
I'm not a circus clown
And you got me down
I'm telling my friends
And telling my fans
Telling my friends
And telling my fans
You got me down
Almost on the ground

The End

Queen Elizabeth

02/27/94

I

Everybody in the street
Everybody on their feet
No need to be discreet
We got a queen to greet
A lady like lady Di
To you, king and I
Only she is that high
And she flew in the sky
If you ask me why
She did it for my guy
She's to me Queen Elizabeth
She went in stealth
It was said he thought of death
A toast to his majesty's health
Across the Atlantic
In London a panic
Filled the pages of the Daily Plant
The brother of Janet
Not from Buckingham Palace
But fear rose like it rose in Dallas
Yet in this land of Toto and Alice
Elizabeth from her western palace
A phone call and she went to him
Long life and prosper Jim
We were on the brim
Of singing a hymn
Is there nothing on your brain?
Do I have to explain?

He landed in pain
Sunshine then rain
Swept through Swingdom
His music magic kingdom
She said I'll risk it all
He must not fall
She saved the brother
Of course we love her
There ain't no other
Brother like this brother
So take your poll
See if prejudice can hold
A lady refined and under control
Her heart was gold
My heart is fleeing
She's a beautiful human being
I thank you Queen
You're one of the finest ladies I have seen
As fine as any Supreme
And you have helped us save our dream
You're Elizabeth the Queen
Queen Elizabeth the Queen
An American Queen
An American Queen
You're Elizabeth the Queen
Queen Elizabeth the Queen
An American Queen
An American Queen

II

For a woman like that
To go for a cat
He's got to be top hat
You get with that
What's that?

I heard he was back
Thinking about a new track
It's rock and black
They couldn't hold her back
Even under attack
On a Mexican trek
She went and brought him back
It was Singapore
Bangkok for sure
He couldn't take anymore
He had to settle the score
But what we didn't know
Because we missed the show
Was that he had an addiction
A prescription affliction
To everything but snow
You gave to him Anglo
At a castle near Hollywood
He faced little Robinhood
So knock on wood
They never understood
The boogie would
The boogie could
Bring to him a lady of good
Joan of Arc from Hollywood
But like that it did
Facing Billy the Kid
I'm not stupid
Forget it cupid
Ain't no love in LA
That's a game they don't play
And if actors have their way
It's do what I say
And so it was
Near Christmas
She filled up at Texaco
Landed in Mexico

The rest I think you know
Isn't she a hero?
Didn't she do the pleading?
She is a beautiful human being
One of the finest ladies I've ever seen
And herself a legend of the big screen
She is Elizabeth the Queen
Queen Elizabeth the Queen
An American Queen
An American Queen
She is Elizabeth the Queen
Queen Elizabeth the Queen
An American Queen
An American Queen

III

Although it wasn't groovy
It could have been a movie
That we didn't foresee
She didn't ask me
She didn't ask you
She was Johnny to the rescue
She went herself
No one saw her when she left
So no one knew
What she was up to
She did what she had to do
She saved the king it's true
So boogaloo it's back you
I celebrate her too
That ain't no maybe
The lady ain't shady
She's one of the real ladies
In or out of her Mercedes
Like him she's top hat

She knows how to act
As a matter of fact
I'm down with that
I'm waiting for his next show
Whenever he says so
That's when I will go
And it's best you know
If you insult the Queen
I'm gonna be mean
Crack your jellybean
I'm on the scene
To honor the Queen
She's the finest lady I've seen
She is the lovely ET
More than a friend you see
She didn't worry about the enemy
She said fight this evil fantasy
It was on her strength that he came back
He was able to stand up against the attack
And ET isn't black
But she had his back
I wish I had a friend like that
Michael is a lucky Cat
Because ET came to bat
And no one else did that
The answers he needed came from her
She helped him through a difficult blur
So no matter what in the future occur
She is the woman we prefer
She is Elizabeth the Queen
Queen Elizabeth the Queen
An American Queen
An American Queen
She is Elizabeth the Queen
Queen Elizabeth the Queen
An American Queen
An American Queen

Chorus

I came to honor the Queen
I came to honor the Queen
I came to honor the Queen
I came to honor the Queen

The End

I'm Just A Double

02/28/94

I

Rick James locked up and forgotten about
James Brown can still dance and shout
Tyson might return but there's no doubt
You and you alone still turn it out
Your life is a tragedy and a song
Surrounded but mostly you are alone
And some have done you wrong
But against evil you must be strong

II

They tried to mess up Doctor King
It was the FBI with their "plant a ho sting"
It was a shame and a low down thing
They hate the sound of the name king
And now with the King of Pop thing
With everybody wanting to hear him sing
Most love to see him do his thing
But some out there wanna crash his reign

III

I love him first because he's me
He has always worked hard to be
That's how it is with folk like me
Born to be but never truly free
But he's got that world respect

I'm here to serve and protect
And I won't stand for disrespect
They're garbage collectors and garbage collectors collect

IV

If Prince Charles was somehow in this
Would they hound him—so there it is
Just say they won't and we'll know how it is
They do dirty laundry but they won't do his
You can be born royal or create the way
Inherit a throne or take it by conquest one day
But to have it because it's what the people say
His fans are the reason he's a king today

V

In only one world do we have the power
The power found in the midnight hour
The kingdom is like a spring shower
Bees spreading pollen off the sunflower
The king is our contact with the source
Through him we maintain love of course
He's driven by love and love is the force
That shall destroy the evil and remorse

VI

He can't live with such bitterness
He can't survive too much belittle-ness
He's the soul and the living witness
He's highly significant to the business
From heaven to hell an angel fell
Los Angeles is a city where that angel dwell
A city west of a world going to hell
If we lose our king we lose our warmth as well

VII

He's special and we all know this to be true
I can't turn my back on him or do
Something dirty to hurt him like you would do
He would never allow me close if that he knew
He's a guy with the truest kind of soul
Not of the now but of the days of old
Reincarnated once a knight to fight the dark patrol
A fight that goes on beyond common observation or
    control

VIII

What does it matter to have great wealth
If it cost you your spiritual health
Who can you trust in the world not to be stealth?
The spy technologies can haunt you to death
And when you find someone pure and good
Monsters are created somewhere in Hollywood
False angels like the knights in white hood
They falsely accuse to destroy the greater good

IX

I don't know the whole story yet
I didn't buy the pain or the debt
Nor did I go to Vegas for the bet
And really truly all I am is upset
But I see no darkness in his eyes
And the eyes have the clearest ties
How can an angel's eyes tell lies
And drive the devil from the skies?

X

If people all over the world love him so
How can we punish him when we don't know?
It seems to me that my people need a hero
Somebody who is not just another zero
I'll stand by him to the end
Like Liz I'll be a true friend
I got nothing to lose but the time I spend
Until the end I will be a friend

XI

Now I have said all I'm gon' say about this
For the moment and from this minute I'm his
So don't push me—my anger is not like his
He won't avenge but I can't handle this
This meanness just to be mean to someone
He forgives but that's not how it's done
Some only understand the gun
If you hit me then buddy you'd better run

XII

Don't seek my help if you can't control it
Remember you're the one that sold it
The man's private life you stole it
But now that darkness has came you can't hold it
He's got to come through for all his fans
He's got to give it up if the kingdom commands
He must and will always play the grandstands
The life of a true performer belongs to the fans

Chorus

I'm just a double stand in for trouble
I'm just a double stand in for trouble
I'm just a double stand in for trouble
I'm just a double stand in for trouble

The End

All Honor To the Queen

03/02/94

I

Let me say it once again
You know the trend
Blood suckers to the end
The one without sin
Cast the first stone
Or leave him alone
And don't say this attack
Ain't because he's black
Young white girls in fact
Are crazy about his act
And you cops can't handle that
That's where y'all are at
Who me? I'm just a fan
A fan at his command
One of the millions who love him
And glad to be one of them
So welcome to the scene
The honor is for the queen
One of the most beautiful ever seen
Herself a legend of the big screen
And been that way since seventeen
With her glamour is routine
I'm talking about her majesty
The lovely, beautiful ET
The one we most wanna see
Including the king and me
I'm saying thank you Liz
For being the lady you is

A dear friend of his
A friend since he starred in the Wiz
Long before Nemo and Walt Diz
From a child he's been in the biz

II

So stand up on your feet
Say we won't retreat
Until victory is complete
Up and down the street
This lady we place over Di
You're our symbol why
You helped save our guy
While others ran on by
You didn't sit home and cry
You went to him and said fight the lie
So if someone asks you why
You loved him cause he's a good guy
All honor to Elizabeth
She didn't go stealth
She didn't fear the tabloids of death
And she wasn't after fame or wealth
And she wasn't in the best of health
Thank you Elizabeth
In the spirit of Snow White
Lady you're all right
Isn't she out of sight?
Now to you tabloid parasite
Write what you gon' write
We know it's out of spite
Like I've said we're ready to fight
And will 'til we bring back the light
I'll bet parasites prefer night
That's why they're so uptight

And so they deal in fright
But Michael and Liz are full of light

III

We're here for the queen
She's a real human being
Talk show host she's not like you
She's not ugly like you
You made the booboo
By catching thirty two
You put him in your lock up zoo
And now you're spreading taboo
You want me to repeat it
Yeah just beat it
Before I make you eat it
Yeah just beat it
Hate is what you got going on
But love is strong
And won't be made to go wrong
That's Michael's song
Understand me dude
If you keep on acting rude
I will conclude
Eliminate your bad attitude
Someone needs to help you
But that's only my view
Another is to knock the hell out of you
That's really what I wanna do
And will if you talk bad about the Queen
I'll get ugly and I'll get mean
I'll crack your jellybean
I've trained so it's routine
So keep your dirty mouth clean
This could become an ugly scene

We're here for the queen
She's a real human being

Chorus

All right all honor to the queen
All right all honor to the queen
All right all honor to the queen
All right all honor to the queen
He's a king and she's a queen
Let's recognize her for being a real human being
He's a king and she's a queen
Let's recognize her for being a real human being

The End

The Lord Work In Mysterious Ways

03/04/94

I

I'm not gon' turn my back
On another white black attack
And pretend that's not what it is
And that the fault is all his
I can see a setup as good as you
And smell the rotten stuff too
Why is he accused of being funny
Is it because he's a black with a lot of money?
I don't give a rip about what they say on TV
He's got too much world popularity
This kid was in like Flint
Ain't nothing about him in print
The law protects him and that's the way
It is with the law in LA today
If he wanted to play a rough part
He could cut straight through to the heart
And so it is a perfect killing
A killing without any blood spilling
A kind of negative exposure homicide
A slow sure death from wounded pride
So they did him and he almost died
It's just money so you decide
Now back to the best of the real thing
The man is still to us the Pop King

II

Now what they don't understand
Is that we won't give up command
And we're willing to take a stand
For the man from Neverland
There are many like me
Who believe in his majesty
What else could he be?
His army of songs keeps setting us free
If you don't believe me finish the book
Don't be a coward take a look
His fame can't simply be took
Not by crook or Captain Hook
In Neverland time stands still
All you got to be is for real
We know it's not just a money deal
There's plenty hatred still
I really think we're on the brink
Of a disaster if you just think
That was a strange earthquake in LA
Maybe God does have something to say
And he's saying listen people okay
I've had enough so hands off of MJ
You know the devil he won't listen to the truth
He'll use you and me and he's used the youth

III

If all we got to do is feed the media's appetite
Hell we all can become rich overnight
All we got to do is get into the treasure house
Hang out at Disney and kidnap Mickey Mouse
It's easy to do the CIA can teach you how
The KGB too if they are still in Moscow
I really think our very next step

Is to write the President for help
All these people want is get to Neverland
And take it from our precious Peter Pan
The kid's been trained and they're sure that they can
They just want the money—isn't that right my man?
And they don't care what they got to do to get it
They'll use the law and they'll break us up wit' it
Why not rob the world's biggest superstar
Drive up like a diplomat—get him in a car
They don't care about the good he's doing all over the
    world
It's the money that's all if he's a Duke of Earl
After they get the dough they'll go away
You won't hear anymore from them okay
Hell America believes in dirt and sells it all the time
In fact you can say this kind of dirt is a gold mine
As long as he is willing to go for the monkey shine
If not they'll play the Press and he'll be convicted of a
    crime

IV

So you see it's quite easy anyone can be misled
Do you believe Oswald shot the president dead?
And James Earl Ray who was just a cheap crook
Got caught overseas and they didn't have to look
And the dope that's now killing us everyday
Wasn't it helped and brought here by the CIA?
I hated the Nazis because they sacrifice'
Millions of Jews, it was an awful human price
In fact I'm sure they suffered greatly
But still I can't approve of what Israel's been doing lately
The West Banks is like Warsaw or a concentration camp
They're shooting so every day there's a new funeral lamp
For many-many years there was no Israel
And now with guns she says let's make a deal

While Arab blood lost through all the crusades
Has bleached the land regardless of these new nationhood
    parades
I feel for Gaza but when a young man comes up out of the
    ghetto
And becomes a world acclaimed who by birth is a Negro
Who can touch the hearts of the world's young
Not with threats of terror but with music and song
I think of how Jesus didn't come with an army but with
    kind-ness and love
In every way he was a poet not a conqueror from above
So I'm saying to the hate spreader and the warmonger
Martyr him if you will and see if he doesn't rise up
    stronger

Chorus

The Lord works in mysterious ways—Give Him the
    praise
The Lord works in mysterious ways—Give Him the
    praise
MJ is another phrase—Don't worry about this daze
The Lord works in mysterious ways—Give Him the
    praise

The End

I Wanna Shine My Own Light

03/27/94

I

Don't let things make you blind
People aren't always kind
Seek and you shall find
Don't let them blow your mind
It's an awful evil time
To be young and in your prime
Accused of awful crime
But stay—don't lose the rhyme

II

It's a vicious dirty low down thing
He never made himself a king
We gave him the royal ring
And he promised he would sing
So as long as he's the king
No matter what evil might bring
I've sworn allegiance to the king
To pop, rock, soul and swing

III

Call him please by his first name
You know it's not about the fame
And really he makes no real claim
He has always been the same
The king is just another name

Accept what the people proclaim
With names we play the game
And with titles we honor his name

IV

It's not the money with him you see
Because he's really very-very wealthy
But money doesn't make a man free
In fact it can be a kind of slavery
And people do everything –you know—you see
Any and everything to build up a treasury
But he's doing good things and I believe that he
Will continue being blessed Lord by Thee

Chorus

I wanna shine my own light
I wanna do what's right
For the people here tonight
I wanna light my own light
If darkness seizes the light
It'll be dark in the world tonight
But that's okay—that's all right
I wanna shine my own light

The End

The Exhortation

03/27/94

I

You're the light my brother
And you're right my brother
We must love one another
Brother you're like no other
No other brother-brother
When will this world discover
Your sensitivity my brother?
You're so kind my brother
Some hate you for it brother
They live in so much trouble
And trouble is like a bubble
Pressure makes it double
They call you a false lover
Your grave they want to cover
Your truth they want to smother
They hate you my brother
Because of the joy you bring
Because you're wealthy as a king
Because you have the world on a string
Because when you move you swing
Because the people made you king
Because of what happens when you sing
Your spirit is a beautiful thing
Seeing you do your thing
You deserve the ring
And so we've given the ring of the king
You're the king of both pop and swing
And you're to so many everything

They may imprison but you shall reign
We're here for you my king
The King of Pop and swing
Rise up my king and sing
Sing and make us free again
Sing and we all shall win
Let's go way back to when
Motown put you in
Into that old top ten
It was five young men
Number one again and again
J 5 took the world by whirlwind
A domination that would end
But not for you my friend
Your magic will never end

II

When "Off the Wall" came in
You were back in the top ten
And you did it again
When "Thriller" busted in
Evil started way back then
It wanted to end
Your career my friend
I dare not pretend
That you're without sin
Everybody has broken one of the ten
Therefore no man is without sin
So how can you offend?
They want to do you in
Cause you are a world friend
A living, breathing whirlwind
And king you'll be to the end
It's you your majesty
That we come to see

Because you make us feel free
The way we should be
So we thank you your majesty
Now take it from me
And know no insanity
Can stop your humanity
We are yours don't they see
We give ourselves freely
To you your majesty
You've saved the love in me
That's your specialty
Thank God that you're free
And for you loving me
I thank you your majesty
You are no simple wonder
Behind you great drums thunder
Bad emotions go asunder
Ancient anger melts in plunder
The oppressed escape from under
You my prince are a wonder
As your enemies blunder
In treachery to put you under
Our love for you will rise to forever
To the thirty fifth of never
It's what keeps us together
Through stormy weather
Betray you we shall never
We stand on that together
So let your voice lift like a feather
And ride the winds of love forever

III

May you leave us never?
If you're diplomatically clever
They will not sever

Our ties to you for they are forever
And when you get it together
We are ready to fight or whatever
Your suffering has been great
Too great here of late
There's so much hate
And jealousy because you are great
The vultures come but too late
So outside they wait
Beyond Neverland's gate
Dark forces anticipate
Hesitate and procrastinate
And lie and debate
Watching from the void
Where angels fear to trod
But you were sent by God
And though they call you odd
Your voice is like Moses' Rod
You dress so super mod
You're too quick for Polaroid
And as you travel for God
The answers come through
And we will too
We will not let them harm you
I promise you that it's true
Though many have withdrew
From loving God like you do
We can see God's good to you
And He stands by you
He'll see you through
The things that evil tries to do
Seeing you perform I report
Your band as a royal court
Solomon wisdom was wrote
Still for you alone I cast my vote
And history one-day will note
How you did promote

And helped kept peace afloat
Evil will not sink your boat
How strange a slave name
Given without dignity is the acclaim
And grace and glory unto fame
Is yours in this your father's name

IV

You're our shelter from the rain
Our healer of social pain
A breaker of that restrain
Promise us you will come back again
There's nothing you need explain
We promise you will continue to gain
We the fans all over this world
And if you don't have a girl
You have this big blue pearl
You are truly a Duke of Earl
We will stand by you
Do what you gotta do
We know you're true
To the red, white and blue
We are in love with you
As a performer and as a person too
Michael you know what I say is true
You know we love you
And we'll always be true
And we'll prove it to you
Mean roads are up ahead
Some want to see you dead
Want to hear your obituary read
But we're black and we're red
And we're white so full speed ahead
Everybody's blood is red
For whatever cause they bled

We will not be misled
Justice will be done
Under God's great sun
It will be for everyone
And for you too Michael Jackson
We will not quit the fight
Until you have been done right
Until you're back under the spotlight
Where your spirit is so bright
It will bring back the limelight
That's why I have to write
In Heaven there is the might
Believe me God knows what's right
I am if you choose your knight
Ready to defend you against all fright
People all over this rock
Are ready to prevent this shock
We will rock with your rock
We will fix the broken clock
And block by block
The world will take stock
And we won't stop
Until you are again the King of Pop

Bridge

This is an exhortation
From a futuristic inspiration
To make this nation
A nation of salvation
This is an exhortation
In our hearts a celebration
Of his carnation
And we do it with great expectation

Ad Lib

We need a king who will be a force in something—Michael
　　is that king
We need a king—We need a king who has that swing
We need Michael—He's the King of Pop and Swing
We need a king who will be a force in something—Michael
　　is that king

The End

I Said I Feel I Feel All Right

03/25/94

I

All this life inside of me
Never thought I would see
A way to be free
But you came to me
And I could see
In and out of me
A glimpse of God's glory
And with his great story
Finally at last I'm free
Free by his decree

II

I've been hurt many times
And still in-between the lines
I've searched my heart to find
A moment for a peace of mind
Through most of it I was blind
Didn't see most of the time
All the dirt and the grime
The Love I had wasn't mine
Just someone to past the time
While I lived on rhythm and rhyme

III

But now I think that I know
Just how love should go
And I'm telling the old hello
That this time I mean no
I can't take it anymore
Not like I did before
I'm telling good-bye to go
And tell yesterday that I know
Just what I'm living for
I don't need this hurt anymore

IV

Might as well change that appetite
The truth is coming to the light
I got no time to fuss and fight
Wrong isn't gon' never do right
Every day can't be sunny and bright
And I'm tired of being so uptight
Now that I think I see the light
I'm walking out on hurt tonight
In the name of justice I know I'm right
In the end I know the poet will write
That I fought the good fight

Bridge

I said I feel—I feel the feeling and the feeling feels all
    right
I said I feel—I feel the feeling and the feeling feels all
    right
Everything is gonna be all right, uptight and out of sight
I said I feel—I feel the feeling and the feeling feels all
    right

The End

I Believe

03/25/94

I

You take a day to hate
And a moment to love
No matter how long you wait
You can't know what's above
You live and you hesitate
You push and you shove
Hoping to pass through the gate
To the city of love
I believe—I believe that love
That love rules all things
Over peasants and kings
Everybody who swings
To everybody that sings
I believe—I believe it is love
I believe it is love
I believe it is love
Because only love
Can keep the stars shinning above
Because only love
Can be the sacrificial dove
Because only love
Loves like love—I believe it is love

II

When you give your heart
When you do your part
Though it's not always smart

You give a helping start
I believe — I believe it is love
To give up on destruction
To live without corruption
To cause no disruption
To give only good instruction
I believe — I believe it is love
To have forgiveness in your heart
To never make a false start
To go and warm a cold heart
To do more than your part
I believe — I believe it is love
I believe it is love
I believe it is love
I believe it is love
Because love is the strongest force in the universe
Because love will never put itself first
I believe it is love
I believe to save the world we need love

III

To meet every day in a good way
Trying never to go astray
To make love what you say
To strangers on life's highway
I believe — I believe it is love
That will give us the victory
That will save human history
That will let us avoid misery
If love became our majesty
I believe — I believe it is love
That allows families to stay together
That allows lovers to pledge forever
That allows evil the victory never
That makes friendship ours forever

I believe—I believe it is love
I believe it is love
I believe it is love
I believe it is love
Because only love has true divinity
Cause only love can grant us serenity
I believe it is love
I believe I believe it is love

Bridge

I believe—I believe—I believe that there's love in you
I believe—I believe—I believe if you believe in me too
I believe—I believe—I believe in what we can do
I believe—I believe—I believe we can make most good
    come   true
I believe—I believe if we believed in love that's all we need
    to do
I believe—I believe—I believe that there's love in you

The End

I Know You're Confused

03/25/94

I

Do you know why hatred's so strong?
It's because we don't turn love on
Do you know why people feel so alone?
They feel like they don't belong
If we keep talking about the bad things
And keep running over the good things
If we keep killing all the good kings
Then all we'll have is what evil brings

II

If all you do and hear is always bad
The good in the world will see us as mad
If you're homeless you got no pad
If all you do is subtract you will never add
When you depend on people to treat you fair
But you can't find honesty anywhere
When all you can find is poison air
Then every breath will lead to despair

III

When whatever you do keeps getting you hurt
Makes you wanna wallow like a pig in the dirt
When you've tried it all and it doesn't work
Given everything but still seen as a jerk
When you done played your very last friend

And your confidence game is at an end
When you've tried to save but all you do is spend
It's a credit card maze and the game is to pretend

Bridge

I know you're confused but don't let it get you down
I know you're confused but don't let it mess you around
I know you're confused but don't let it drive you
    underground
I know you're confused but don't let it turn you upside
    down
I know you're confused—I know you're confused
But believe we all are confused cause we're all being used

The End

Do You Know and Do You Know the Man

03/28/94

I

I don't care what they think of me
I don't give a rip what they say I ought to be
Cause I know what I am and I am me
I'm not living to prove myself to them
I'm not dumb enough to take chances when chances are
    slim
As far as I'm concerned—forget it Jim

II

Yes I'm down but I'm not out
Been knocked around and talked about
I dance and I'm free to shout
I'll take the hurt and I'll live
Every day is another day for me to give
His love back and that's how I will live

III

So let them talk if they please
They talked about him now they're on their knees
He's the door and he got the keys
I'm going to love the best I can
After all beyond all else I believe in the man
And I wanna be his biggest fan

IV

If you love me well then that's okay
You don't have to listen to what they say
All will be judged on judgment day
If you're here and you're living right
It doesn't matter whose in the spotlight
Everybody gets a chance to do it right

Chorus

Do you know and do you know the man
Do you know and do you know the man
He's the leader—the leader of the band
Do you know and do you know the man
Do you know and do you know the man
He's the leader—the leader of the band

The End

Close To The Edge

Our entertainers, the great ones attract audiences like in the old days the prophets use to do and if they are dynamic enough they seem to foster bigger then life personas. Some almost seem to be spiritual figures with people watching them with unbelievable devotion. Is it possible that entertainers will become our future prophets? Is Michael a vision of what is possible in a world without prejudice and if he is—does he know that he is? My question is how does he see himself in the world? Does he see himself as more than an entertainer and if so what does he see? I only know what I see and that often is confusing to me.

There were hard questions to be asked and answered. Michael had labored so hard to be recognized as a man rather than as a black man, but for struggling blacks that was a problem. His plastic surgery and color change shocked the black community who didn't know what to make of what he was doing. Suddenly he had married twice, each time to a white woman. Considering the surgery, the color change and the marriages, one could propose that a personality preference was beginning to show itself. Michael said he loved his race but everything he did said he didn't. We realized that the majority of his fans now were white and had been since the Jackson Five broke up. Michael's change from R and B to Rock format drastically altered his appeal to black supporters. For him these things were the right things to do but for us they spelled abandonment. Still those who really loved him held on despite their shifting feelings.

I Want To Die Honorably

04/16/94

I

There comes a time when a man would rather die
Than get on his knees before his enemies and cry
There comes a time when a man would rather die
Than suffer the abuses of another outrageous lie
These are such times my friends for you and I
To decide whether to go on cowardly or fight and die
We have given more to this land than any man
And the bounty off that sweat and blood can
And should have paid the cost of freedom we seek
That is why we cannot turn the other cheek
Less our bodies fall to the ground broken and weak
Instead we should rise up and cross the bloody peak
We must use whatever means necessary
For that is what we crave and if need be
We must sacrifice body and soul
Heaven may rule but hell is in control
Of everything beyond heaven's gate
We cannot undergo another unjust wait
There is no honor in second class citizenship
If it's not for them it's not for us this trip
Blood doesn't flow beneath our skin only
Though they may break me they will never again own me
I have readied myself for this scourge and I come not only
Armed with prayer but with the sword of my testimony

II

I smell the funeral fires burning as we hedge for battle
And in that fight my saber from fear will not rattle
I am not on my knees and we will not die like cattle
In brave uproar we will be felt from Boston to Seattle
Destroying those restrains that held us captive and
  coward
So unless we be dead we will not be overpowered
We will not fall by the wayside but look ever forward
Into that bright hope that as blacks we have towered
The heights of indignity and whatever pain the enemy
  brings
Having been slaves when he destroyed our kings
We rise—for centuries we have been tabooed as dark
  things
But the breezes blow onward toward the place where
  victory sings
So for honor we pledge to the death my friend
We will not cower and we will not give up until we reach
  our chosen end
So from this day I promise you that I will spend
Every heartbeat to obtain it even unto the bloody end
How many times have we died in pointless vengeance?
How many times have we been horrid on nothing but a
  glance?
Our saddened eyes flooded and hearts broken by
  circumstance
As monstrous indifference held back our advance
This we are doing to protect our children not yet saluted
That which was is now and in battle constituted
From the long injustice that were once rooted
In the unwritten laws of poverty that cannot be disputed

III

Let no black warrior here die in some foreplay
Before righteous intercourse arms him the right way
There comes a time that a man would rather die
Than be defiled by lesser foes than you or I
There comes a time when a man would rather die
Than yield one moment to be dishonored by a lie
The lie they invented is to prevent our participation in
    this   drama
To convince us that we cannot bear the trauma
But like them I came from the belly of my mama
What a tragic and comedic tale it is to live such a
    melodrama
If this is life it is not what life is supposed to be
I cannot dishonor myself and be prey to a history
That disallows me a chance for a princely victory
In life then I choose death—It is written so let it be
Restrained I once allowed myself to be in servitude
But now I rise in protest with a brand new attitude
I shall regain my African honor no matter how crude or
    rude
I must be to morality and this time I conclude
I will not kiss butt or drink out of a piss filled cup
Or ride behind any that challenge my dignity—I am up
I will not be seduced by nor crippled by personal fear
I will break free from these chains that bind me here
I don't seek nor accept forgiveness because it is a pretense
I will attack any that seek to enslave me or give rise to a
    similar offense

Bridge

I want to die honorably not simply for wealth
I want to die for the honor of a warrior's death
I want to die honorably not simply for health
I want to die for the honor of a warrior's death
I want to die honorably not be a token on a shelf
I want to die for the honor of a warrior's death
I want to die honorably not for you but for myself
I want to die for the honor of a warrior's death

The End

The Same Old Game

04/30/94

I

You take away the king
The king of swing
A symbol to everything
And then you bring
Us back to gangbang
Put us in a gang
That was never his thing
We're selling cocaine
Trying to maintain
All we have is pain
And the miserable kiss
Of the dope bliss
We were out there and you could not miss
You put us on the All-American hit list
There is something wrong with that but this
On the real is how it is
I saw Michael's tears
I know he has fears
I've had them myself for years
While you were drinking beers
Parked at home in front of your TV set
You have no idea of the debt
You owe and you don't understand the bet
If you did you would break out in a sweat
Michael is in trouble man
He's in trouble understand
I haven't seen him wit' a band
But I don't need you to hold my hand

I'm talking about going to the mat
If he needs me to do that
Besides the talk that's where it's at
I know your career is flat
That's exactly what it is
There is nothing stopping us from being his
So it's best that you get down wit' this
As far as the kingdom goes he is all there is

II

They talk about prison life
Wanting to make him the wife
Of some inmate with a knife
So we're faced with this strife
You're not my lawyer— I'm not your client
But I am defiant
And I'm self-reliant
Michael's the giant
I don't want to be violent
But I can no longer be silent
So I'm telling the world
Every woman, man, boy and girl
They can't even climb his beanstalk
They don't understand the moonwalk
Punk you have got to cut it loose
Before someone breaks on you like Bruce
He wants to save our youth
You don't know the truth
Talking to you is like talking to Dr. Ruth
I didn't know you were so damn uncouth
It's hard being a black man
But there won't be another Jackson plan
Yet 'cause he's a rich man
Who has been to the Promised Land
And drinks from a big cup

You come around and start acting up
He's no abandoned pup
That's why you're so stirred up
But we're gonna ride this horse
The hell with your remorse
What we got we will endorse
Their kind of peace pisses me off
I don't wanna play golf
With 'em cause I'm too pissed off

III

They're playing games
Using dirty names
Creating frames
For jump claims
Michael is the acclaim
They have no right to his fame
This disgraceful campaign
That they sustain
Won't stop us from standing in the rain
To see him again
But that isn't the problem
They want to rob him
We want to mob him
I don't have a white girl problem
Don't be a racist
Touch all the bases
All I see is black faces
In their prison places
You know how they start
They break a black heart
Michael is enjoyed
They want him in a void
They want him destroyed
Cause he ain't Caucasoid

Now back to Capital Hill
The new crime bill
Is a way to kill
Inner city will
Brothers I know still
Fight the ordeal
If we ever get control
The poison they sold
Will be used to defeat their goals
We are watching their polls
While they are digging holes
Not for our bodies but for our souls

IV

They say they want the streets
So they're making sweeps
The thing with trouble is it repeats
It comes back on creeps
No I'm not gon' sign their treaty
Or stop my word graffiti
Not as long as the greedy
Take advantage of the needy
I'm talking about the big times
The white collar crimes
Where the dollar sign
Is always the bottom line
If we could steal like they steal
We'd have no reason to kill
So what's the damn deal
If it ain't kill or be killed?
With the brothers on the streets
This behavior is for keeps
Blood runs only if the heart beats
This is a hay day for creeps
Yet and still in gang law

You win or lose but never draw
You don't ride the seesaw
Where drive by is the law
But working in a new campaign
I think I should maintain
That a bullet to the brain
Ain't the thing to sustain
Let's get them against the ropes
Crack their cantaloupes
But if we have to cope
With losing we won't lose hope
We want Michael back
We believe this attack
Is against him because he's black
It's another day of field and track

Chorus

Three strikes you're out—That's the old game—The new
    game is the same
All they've changed is the name and that's the old game—
    The   new game is the same
All they've changed is the name—It's still the same old
    game
It's three strikes you're out and we play it because we're
    insane but that's the game

The End

Could He Be Convicted

05/07/94

I

The moment I heard
What had occurred
Before I conferred
I reached for my sword
But all I could afford
Was a nail in a board
The media came in
To witness for sin
How could he win
Come back again
Money will spend
But I got none to send
It looked like the end
For my famous friend
I had never met him
But I couldn't forget him
What would they do wit' him?
Trying to get him
They took every shot
And all they got
Was the benefit of the doubt
They couldn't turn him out
Yet all we do is go about
While they have we live without
So we dance and shout
We have nothing but still they pout
How can we do better?
When we can't get together

It's sunny but it's still foul weather
It's hot but I'm wearing my leather
They're trying to destroy his career
They're doing it by using this awful smear
You're damn right I fear
I've got fear like all his fans everywhere

II

Day after day I waited
Tortured so much I faded
But the way they played it
Because he made it
He would be degraded
They wanted his wealth traded
They hated his rich lifestyle
They talk about it to beguile
And while they smiled
All I could do was wait awhile
They said what they said
They pulled off their raid
After which I was afraid
How did he let himself get betrayed?
So he had it made
But it wasn't 'til after the first grade
Before that the bills barely got paid
J 5 had to make it in the trade
A life on the road
Was a heavy load
For a young boy
Who had a rat as a toy
He's too sensitive to destroy
What had he done to that boy
I didn't know and didn't care
It was his pain I wanted to share
He was being smeared

Halfway around the world cheered
Before the smoke cleared
He simply disappeared
My heart then freezing froze
But it was pleasing to some Negroes
They said he was one of those
So called wanna be white black pros

III

With all my perplexes
About the shot in Texas
The Os and the Xs
Said the attack wasn't sexist
I was spending days my friend
Hoping it would end
I feared so much by then
I started to pretend
That he knew me
But how would he do me
If he really knew me
Could he look through me
Like I wasn't there?
How could a guy like that care?
He was all over the world and I was nowhere
I guess I wanted a share
Of his life and I didn't care
About the cops or the smear
I pretended he was near
I could see myself standing there
Waiting on the last bell
I would go wit' him through hell
Or up in heaven if he hadn't fell
After all it was my fairy tale
It was the only thing I dreamed
The only thing I schemed

The only thing and it seemed
If I prayed he'd be redeemed
So I sent love and waited for it to be returned
I learned all that could be learned
Long ago my loyalty he'd earned
My feelings were hot for him so they burned

Bridge

With all my thoughts restricted
Everything I believed contradicted
All my private dreams afflicted
Could he be convicted— Could he be convicted?
Questioning all I just tried to kick it
And tell them where they could stick it
Okay guitar player—go head pick it
Could he be convicted— Could he be convicted?

The End

Some Say I Got A Nerve

Undated

I

You're buying hope—hoping to be left alone
You got to be strong
The way they're after you they wanna get it on
They wanna do you wrong
But where much money is made
You know the trade
I can't tell you how long I've stayed
Hidden in the shade
But now that I'm up to grade
I got to get played
I got to get paid
But I don't want you to fade
You're still my choice
The sound of my voice
Clears all the noise
Left by the good old boys
But know they can do me where I set
But I'm not gon' forget
That you're the king for whom I sweat
I don't think I will regret
Blowing what for them is an opportunity
When you've already paid for immunity
From prosecution or are you fooling me
Shouldn't you be schooling me?
Let it hit me
Let it git me
Let me git down wit' it—still
The real power is the dollar bill

And like others I need to refill
I know words can kill
But a man of your strength, determination and will
Will never to evil yield

II

Responsibilities I got my share
It ain't that I don't care
You're known everywhere
You're a multimillionaire
One day you'll be a billionaire
And I'll still be here
A poor man why should you fear
Me riding this smear?
I mean what you think
I'm just trying to get to the bank
Just trying to get out of red ink
But I ain't foolish enough to yank
On no big dog's chain
I'm simply trying to ride this train
Someplace out the rain
You're a hurricane
When you perform
You create a storm
You're never lukewarm
And with that great charm
You drop the bomb
You make us numb
You make us overcome
Our frustrations like a mighty drum
You've been freer than most
You blew minds like the Holy Ghost
I'm bragging but you don't need my boast
You're legendary coast to coast
And all over the world

You could have any girl
You rock this world
Who me? I'm just a squirrel

III

I've wanted to be your friend a long time
Back before your prime
Long before they accused you of a crime
You were ringing my chime
I don't know what you think is a disgrace
But I'm proud of my race
I'm not changing my face
I don't have your power base
But I can understand
Because of world demand
You wanna be universal if you can
I'm still gon' be your fan
I'm not a saint
You won't hear a complaint
Even if you wear white paint
Understand I can't
Change my color—I will always be black
If that means I'm going to be held back
I will have to deal with that
I'm not like you a top cat
I don't have the fans you do
Few in the world have as many followers as you
And attention and review
Are old hat to you but to me they are brand new
If what I say shocks you
I mean if it really rocks you
That's not what I'm trying to do
I wouldn't think of hurting you
But I got a craft too
I'm doing what I have to do

And besides that I'm keeping it true
Just like you would if you had to

Chorus

Some say I got a nerve
Cause I'm trying to serve
I didn't throw a curve
I'm not trying to perturb
You're still the king
You still got game
You're still everything
True to your father's name

The End

Do You Wanna Be White

I thought about the next piece a lot. It comes down to one thing, We are afraid of losing Michael. Afraid he is no longer us. We as a people don't have much and to lose an artist of his magnitude would be devastating. His transformations left us unsettled, searching for answers we did not have. Why would he deny us the one thing we could claim, his blackness? He said he was black and proud of it but the color change, the marriages and the surgery said different. Were we to believe his words or his actions? "Do You Wanna Be White" as painful as it was to write puts that question in plain sight. Though I fear upsetting Michael I can't hide from my own heart. Let me point out that the poem has nothing to do with white people being white. It has to do with blacks being black. It has to do with us losing another hero, one that we can't afford to lose. Michael has an awesome presence in the world, even after the debacle he's been through; he is still awesome. We are still trying to hold on, still trying to keep him to ourselves, selfish yes, but we do love him and we can always make the claim that we nurtured him first.

I think that if we had known about the Vitiligo before the treatment, the transformation would have been more wildly accepted. We didn't know and when face to face with the results it frightened us. Regardless of our astonishment, Michael is not a liar and reluctantly I have grown to accept the color change as a treatment rather than a preference. Still the poem focuses on questions I face every time I mention his name. And it's not just blacks that ask them they are universal. Many white long time supporters are puzzled just like the black ones are. For me it's an every day problem and everyone who knows me knows how vigilant I am in my support for Michael. I don't think black or white makes a person worthy but the history of the relationship between our races says it does. So once again it is not Michael's preferences I'm dealing with but my own. A point of interest: consider your child growing up and becoming progressively different from you and the changes are producing strain. Remember the Michael of the early eighties compared the Michael you see today. The storm of who or what he is—is always a hurricane for me and I've been swept out to sea and lost many times.

There is a young girl with Vitiligo where I work and she looks like a burn victim. It is very disfiguring and noticeable. If Michael's problem came close to looking like hers then I fully understand and accept why he had treatment to remove the pigmentation from his skin. However since imagery is extremely important to black people I still think he should've told us about the problem before he had the treatment. This poem is a reaction to a transformation that we simply didn't understand. But I want it known that even with our expressed indifference we have and do love him. We have to ask can we hate oppression and not hate the oppressor. Are we free now? What happens if one of us over achieves and winds up rich and successful? Do we start looking for things to bring that person down? Are we looking at a treatment result or the manifestation of too much isolation?

Undated

I

Though you have our trust
I must ask—are you ashamed of us
Still that doesn't change the fact
That you are genetically black
No matter how white your skin or act
You can't change that fact
Even if you turn your back
You will always be black
Your offspring will be black

The way you dance and sing will be black
Would you have came under attack
If you had not been black?
Even if you're the world's biggest star
Black ain't how but what you are
No matter what other races you attract
You can't change a genetic fact
Suppressing your melanination
Or escaping UV radiation
May alter the way you look but the black nation
Has made no declaration
Against you nor have we betrayed you
Remember who made you
Remember who paid you
Remember who first played you
I can't say you didn't deserve it because you did
We have been with you since you were a kid
So don't treat us like we're stupid
Turning white won't make you cupid
No wonder you got the trouble you got
Got hit with a cheap shot
We were not asked to visit Camelot
But we were first to recognize you're hot

II

I mean I could see the attack
Was related to the fact you got stack
And I'm not gon' turn my back
Because you don't wanna be black
All I know my brother
Is that we're killing each other
But before you become one of them brother
Remember what you told your mother
Before you decided to lose your racial ID
Look like them instead of looking like me

It could make you strange and ugly
A man can be cute but never lovely
You can sign your name with an X
And declare that you're a unisex
I can only ask what's next
Aren't you out of context?
The things you told Oprah I believed
Like millions of others was I deceived?
You had the world on a string
And you performed from center ring
You danced and you could sing
And we crowned you our king
And now it seems that you don't wanna hang
Are you involved with a white only gang?
We're your subjects—have you brought us to shame
We still hold you higher than blame
We came out to support your name
We offered you fortune and fame
They're around you now but they ain't who I am
Ain't dedicated to you through your world of jam

III

We're a people divested of economic powers
The little we have seldom is ours
Our children have turned to rocks and powder
With every voice we have our protest is louder
And then God sends us someone like you
Who can do what most of us cannot do
So we lift you up high until the world sees you
Until it knows what black genius can do
Through it all we've been faithful and true
Through it all we've shown that we love you
And we were so proud and now we hurt
For you have arrived and cast us off like dirt
Your response to our loyalty and devotion

Has been devoid of real black emotion
You bath your body with skin lightening lotion
Everything you do seems to reflect the notion
That you don't wanna be black
When that's all you are in fact
Upon our lives you've had a great impact
And though you can we will not turn our back
You say you belong to the world now
You perform in places like Moscow
And maybe through your magic somehow
You have broken forever the role behind the plow
Maybe you have truly risen to the rank of royalty
Is that a reason for your disloyalty?
I do not question your sovereignty
I do question your reason for ditching me
I know we're violent and that's up front
But compared to those you copy that's a mute point

Chorus

We're not the one who are saying that you wanna be white
The whites are saying that you wanna be white—all right
We're not the ones who are saying that you wanna be
    white
The whites are saying that you wanna be white—all right
All right—all right—all right—Do you wanna be white
We're not the one who are saying that you wanna be white
The whites are saying that you wanna be white—all right
    all right—are they right?
Tell me brother do you wanna be white
Tell me do you wanna—do you wanna—wanna be white

The End

Marriages and Bloodline Comments

Michael's first marriage was to show the world that he was normal and that he could have a serious relationship with a woman. But it shouldn't have been with a rich little spoiled girl who had already been in one marriage. Michael hadn't had a lot of exposure to women on an intimate level before his relationship with Marie. Because he had deep religious commitments he was a kept man and that was because it condemned sex before marriage and his busy schedule and work commitment reduced opportunity to find someone which he could have had such a relationship. Skepticism also played a role in what seem to be an avoidance pattern.

Why didn't the marriage between Lisa and Michael work out? They both were young handsome extremely rich people who had everything going for them—so why didn't they stay together? If Michael's sexuality hadn't been a speculated item the situation involving his being with a woman wouldn't have came up? Was she an escape for Michael who was being pressure to the extreme about how he felt about women? Here was a guy that almost any young affluence woman in the world would have been overjoyed to have been with yet he chose a woman with two children who had already been married to marry. That choice alone with the questions about his sexuality led to some interesting speculation about what happened between them. And the poems concerning LMP are speculations. She didn't marry him for money. She understood the drug problem he had successfully been treated for because her father had had one. It was reported that she greatly loved children and having come from a Hollywood background there was nothing about his life as an entertainer that could have been first hand or surprise to her. She was a very rich attractive woman. He was a very rich attractive man. One would have easily thought it was a marriage made in heaven yet their time together was very short. Was the break up due to the fact that she couldn't have children and Michael more than his own life wanted children? Was that the reason but Michael knew before the marriage that she couldn't have children so why did he involve himself in a situation doomed from the start?

His second marriage was another mystery especially to black people some of whom were saying that he wanted to be white. They asked: "Why couldn't he have chosen a black woman?" But he had no exposure to the community of black women and must I say I believe he feared getting that exposure. The only fault I find is that he could've went to his brothers and they could have introduced to him to a safe choice. But he wound up with a nurse from one of his doctor's office. I'm sure she idolized Michael and probably tried to measure up. But Michael is a perfectionist and I don't know if any woman can meet all his particulars. But at least out of this marriage two children were born to him and that's something he has wanted all of his adult life.

Michael Was Born Thirty Some Years Ago

09/11/96

I

I believe I remember when it was
It was almost Christmas
The law said your statement cuz
Do you wanna play da duz
We don't care who your mama is or was
But if they don't who does
What I'm saying MJ
Is don't be too concerned about what people say
You have got to let your music play
Every night and every day 'til they forget this MJ
Let 'em do what they will
Nobody has got your skill
Nobody can deal like you deal
To your fans that's what's real
They will never break our loyalty
They can steal your royalty
They can crush your sovereignty
These punks have that authority
MJ that's my word
So give them the third
You know the almighty bird
Let me tell them if they haven't heard
He don't want to talk to you
So screw your interview
Fool what y'all gon' do
Get his sick sister too
Do you want her to sing for you?
Do you want her to give you the do-do?

Back to the royal court
Everybody cast your vote
And please-please denote
I'm putting aggressors on report
Send me a financial quote
Welcome to the Neverland Fort

II

So what you think I know
About Michael's Vitiligo
He could get as white as snow
Or be a straight albino
You know he's what they call recluse
Look what happened when he cut loose
You ran him like you ran the Juice
You almost had a deuce
Both in jail at the same time
Both charged with a crime
All I got for you is my rhyme
He's the one that can spin on a dime
Sure he was married to L.M.P. for awhile
But she cramped his style
He's not ease to beguile
She had that little rich girl smile
But hidden in the depth of her eyes
You could see compromise
Never at home—she had her alibis
But Michael had fought lies
So that ended his thing with Marie
All she wanted was a movie
And a spot on MTV
And fans across the sea
She kept saying you promised me
Now produce my CD
And he might've in time did it

But she kept hitting him wit' it
Janet liked her they say
Still that had to end one-day
Because between JJ and MJ
Blood is blood is blood okay

III

You know my feelings are mixed about him
Sometimes I talk about him
Negatively and I doubt him
I never thought of living my life without him
There's not a day that goes by
That I don't think about him why?
Well all I can say is he's my guy
Maybe I'm disturbed because he's whiter than I
I don't understand why he did it so
But neither do I know about Vitiligo
But I hope it's not a mental syndrome
They say it's because of a bad chromosome
If I could get him on the phone
I would ask but he's no drone
He thinks everything through
But I think it might be true
That he wants to be a universal man
To be of no particular race if he can
Truly to be the first human Peter Pan
Maybe that's why he bought Neverland
And though I don't appreciate the look
I'm not gon' be another Captain Hook
I'm not gon' help his enemies make book
I'm not gon' be their rook
My disappointment I have expressed
The many times I have addressed
That issue and others in this story
I've never tried to cheat him of his glory

I've never invaded uncharted territory
I've done my best to tell his great story

Chorus

Michael was born thirty some years ago
To a station that some say is low
He was born an American Negro
Michael was born thirty some years ago
Became the greatest pop star the world would know
He was one of the proud sons of Katherine and Joe
Michael was born thirty some years ago as a Negro
Michael was born thirty some years ago

The End

I'm Talking About You Know LMP

Undated

I

Suddenly there was a situation
That led to speculation
After his deepest penetration
Did he satisfy her starvation
For a big strong man?
Which he wasn't you understand
Because without his band
He was just an ordinary man
But put him on a stage
And allow him to engage
He will create a rage
He will make Front-page
Not that he couldn't blow her mind
He does that worldwide all the time
If you look at him you will find
The guy is more than rhyme
He is extremely kind
He dresses super fine
His feelings aren't blind
Why wouldn't he attract a woman's mind?
He's a dancing machine
He's neat and very clean
Everybody loves his routine
He's got all kinds of green
He's nice to look at
But he keeps changing that
So what if that's a fact
He's got the top act

And may be suffering from panic attack
I don't know I ain't got that much jack
In fact I'm kind of slack
But I'm glad that he is black

II

If you were rich you understood
How really dawn good
Life was in Hollywood
But not if you were from the hood
So the trouble was over
He was once again sober
How much time did it take to discover
That he needed a lover?
Did he ask his mother?
Did he talk to a brother?
Why? Because they trust one another
Why did he need this lover?
I know he was lonely
He'd signed with Sony
And he's no phony
But to choose a one and only
Make you think there was something to discuss
It wouldn't have been a violation of her trust
Her father grew up where we rode the back of the bus
He could have but he didn't befriend us
How did we feel about him?
Let's say he was one of them
But he was a rock and roll gem
So like God we had to love him
What was her childhood like?
Did she ride her bike?
Did she know about Tina and Ike?
Did she love the Mike?
These are questions we don't have the answers to

So I'm stuck with the old voodoo
Not that I'm trying to put a jinks on you
Sometimes you can't escape the old taboo

III

And no one knew it see
They married secretly
The first time I knew was on TV
I kept saying how could this be?
But I knew he would never ask me
After all the man was free
To choose his own destiny
What I was thinking the hell with me
Okay she was kind of fine
From a very important line
And in the back of my mind
I believed she was sweet and kind
So why should I oppose her
After all he chose her?
And he's the one who knows her
Yes I suppose her
Time with him was great
Any woman would hate
To miss out on such a date
To miss out on such a fate
There intimate lives I don't know
You know he never said so
Gave us only one video
So my imagination did grow
If it lied I'm not sure?
Am I sick do I need a cure?
Have I been too premature?
What did he really endure?
What about the things I've said?
Yes I am very afraid

Hurt him I would rather be dead
But I had to get it out of my head

Chorus

She probably loved him initially
I'm talking about you know LMP
But was it a condition that he
In the fullness of time and reality
Simply seeing could not see
Simply being could not let be
I'm talking about you know LMP
And the things we did not see

The End

Separation Was Inevitable

Undated

I

When I got up this morning when
I heard the decision was in
I started to count to ten
I had something to transcend
I hope the prenuptial was strong
That you did it like you would a song
Then it won't catch you wrong
But that depends on where you belong
You said don't color you black or white
You didn't wanna be seen in that light
But you know right is right
That's not Press bias or appetite
No matter which way they write
You're black in their sight
So be it wrong or right
That's how they see you tonight
You know she only suppose
She was never really yours
She wanted your prose
She wanted you to compose
You knew she was a prickly little rose
The first time she took off her clothes
Leaves, petals and bows
Only for a moment was she yours

II

Now did you ever suppose?
Some people use Negroes
In games they propose
Why only heaven knows?
We have sisters don't we bros.
In our race every color shows
The difference heaven knows
'Cause only heaven can compose
And that beauty glows and grows
Even in places where it snows
The contrast of the black rose
Make cupids break their bows
They lose their arrows
But now that your skin is so white
Perhaps you have lost that Inner Light
That spiritual deep insight
And you're sleeping alone tonight
I must admit to satire
Because you could've had a sapphire
A dark and lovely fire
To fit your body attire
To fulfill your lust and desire
To give you love 'til you expire
This woman was already a used fire
She was hot but she's no black wire

III

My question is have you chose
Not to wear on your clothes
Your colored ribbons and bows
You know we love those
But for a prickly white rose
To be worn like a pin on your clothes

You know that's gon' anger Negroes
Who have been with you since your bros.
And you broke up long ago
Looks like you're anti Negro
I know you don't know
But that's the way it looks though
You see my king it's not the rock you do
It's because you labor to be true
That's why the young are endeared to you
And of course you rock them too
Just remember we wanted you way back
When your skin was darker black
Fans don't care about this attack
They just want their Michael back
Every record and every track
That you produced has had an impact
They wanna stay in contact
They really want you back
They don't care if you're blacker than black

Chorus

Separation was inevitable
You were gullible
But God made you indelible
Please stay available
Separation was inevitable
But God made you indelible
You are incredible
But not infallible
Please stay available
Available-available-available

The End

She's The Daughter of A King

07/08/96

I

Not long before I gained sight
Into what I would write
And oh I was so full of fight
Aware I began to recite
Michael it's all right
Make me your first knight
I dreamed of Camelot
But the woman that you have got
She interests me not
I won't be your Sir Lancelot
But for you she may be the shot
But in her heart she loves you not
Her love is too high price
Even if you want to be nice
We're no longer traded for spice
She will never make the sacrifice
She has got a vice
She ain't that nice
But she's your wife
And as a knight I'll protect her with my life
Though I think you married on poor advice
One day she could rob you of your paradise
Michael she ain't that nice
She seems warm but she's as cold as ice
And now she's been married twice
Maybe she likes to roll the dice
I don't think you sought your mom's advice
Your relationship with this woman is on ice

On plain earth you may be the salt
But when this stuff hits the asphalt
You will see it will be all-your fault
And you'll be victimized by another assault

II

I know you think its talk
That she will never walk
But if the dead are outlined in chalk
If every pitcher who hasn't will balk
Love can't be taught
It ain't love that you have caught
No matter what you thought
A woman like that can't be bought
And though you can try
And though you can buy
Her pieces of the apple pie
That girl's price is too high
She's got that evil eye
She's gon' hurt you guy
You know I don't lie
She just wanna occupy
A piece of your stage
A piece of your wage
A piece of your age
A piece of front page
Soon you will feel her rage
If you don't share with her your stage
She don't want the other proposal
You'll be at her disposal
I don't know the disclosure
But I can see the exposure
Of things you can't see
She's over twenty-one, white and free
She's another king's daughter

And if you think you've caught her
You weren't the one who taught her
She'll leave you or lead you to the slaughter

III

I know her daddy hung around
On back streets in N word town
He was getting it down
Preparing to take the black sound
First into the white underground
Where his kind were found
But luck had him superstar bound
And no doubt he earned his crown
He was white and he sounded black
And did it way back
He was poor from across the track
Then he bought that pink Cadillac
I'm not trying to down the Cat
But you know we do that
That's part of our cultural act
That's us in spirit and fact
Still he established the contact
And had a great impact
On you getting to where you're at
I know you respect that
But understand his little girl
Didn't grow up as he did in this world
She grew up with diamonds and pearls
With American Duchesses and Earls
And with money like Exxon got oil
You have to expect she will recoil
If you can't resolve it she's spoiled
And she has never toiled
And so this is what girls like her do
She might've thought she wanted you

Because you were fresh and new
But she will lay an old fashion hurt on you

Chorus

Come on now y'all and sing
She's the daughter of a king
Come on now y'all and sing
She's the daughter of a king
Come on now y'all and sing
She's the daughter of a king
She's a poisoned little thing
She's the daughter of a king

The End

You Know You Don't Mean Him No Good

11/22/95

I

You know you don't mean him no good
You're gon' cut his throat
Throw him off the boat
Just to see if he will float
Love can be a cement overcoat
You know you don't mean him no good
Every since that kid
He's been mostly hid
And it may sound stupid
But he believes in cupid
You know you don't mean him no good
You can't love each other
You're gon' hurt this brother
He should've asked his mother
They love each other
You know you don't mean him no good
I know it ain't about money
He married you to prove he wasn't funny
In Hawaii was it sunny?
You were over there with another honey
You know you don't mean him no good

II

You know you don't mean him no good
He was a kid from the hood
Who went out and made good
Even from where you stood

He was special in Hollywood
You know you don't mean him no good
So what record deal did you cut?
What did he pay for your butt?
All I see you do is strut
He married you because he was in a rut
You know you don't mean him no good
He's always lived in a fairy tale
He's been through his first taste of real hell
And now you ring the bell
Starting to rattle your tail
You know you don't mean him no good
Did he promise you show biz fame?
That he would promote your name
Put you in your father's game
Since he didn't it ain't the same
You know you don't mean him no good

III

You know you don't mean him no good
How did he get in this mess
Promoting the talent-less?
Girl you're at his address
And now you wanna protest?
You know you don't mean him no good
Even though he's universal
That doesn't mean you'll be commercial
You know no prenuptial
Is gon' make you special
You know you don't mean him no good
Blackness ain't a put on
It's too deep to the get on
That's why he gets it on
But it ain't lipstick you can put on
You know you don't mean him no good

Is that the way y'all do in Hollywood?
Just because he acts like Robin hood
Goes around the world and tries to do good
You're using him like some said you would
You know you don't mean him no good

Chorus

What you want is outrageous
Even though he's courageous
What you want is outrageous
Even though he's courageous
What you want is outrageous
He doesn't owe Los Vegas
And you're not contagious
What you want is outrageous

The End

You Are the Son of the King

03/25/97

I

I wonder little PJ
Will you come and sing for us one-day
I know you can't walk
I know you can't talk
I know you're just a baby boy
And you give your father so much joy
And we share in his happiness
All those years alone he's been in this
Kingdom in the mist
And now joyfulness
Has filled that empty abyss
He has a new baby to kiss
And you're naturally his
Nothing for him could be greater than this
And so I reminisce
Wondering if you too will be on the hit list
I want his kingdom to go on
He named you Prince that can't be wrong
Maybe like your father you'll be well known
I have to say my feelings for him are strong
I only hope that you will carry on
The traditions of your father's throne
But more importantly I hope you'll grow up strong
And be like him when you get grown

II

Prince I have watched your father's recovery from afar
Against those who wanted to tarnish his star
I have never met him but I hope that won't be always
As I set here in this forward glaze
Recanting all of the ways
And times I prayed—so many days
For him—he has influenced my life
I feared when he took his first wife
And when he took the second one
I became quite undone
The battle he was fighting had not been won
The great name of Michael Jackson
Was still in the shadows of many minds
And the giver of signs
Had not lifted the blinds
And the darker kinds
Of thoughts were following him
Though I never accepted them
They were always around
Trying to bring him down
I wondered if happiness would ever be found
Fifteen years after Motown
And years after he had received the crown
They made him out to be some freaky clown
And his world was tumbling down
But finally I think his heart has rebound

III

And now there is wonderful little you
His first born long over due
There's just him, your mother and you
And a kingdom that has tried to stay true
That will one day belong to you

If that is what you choose to do
May God bestow his blessings upon you?
And upon your mother and father too
May he lift you up the way he lifted your dad?
Remember always Thriller and I'm Bad
As you climb aboard the launching pad
And sail among the stars charted by your dad
And happiness will abound
If you carry forth the crown
Blazing the galaxies around
Created because your father added beauty to sound
Tomorrow you'll travel to the stars
Perhaps long past Jupiter and Mars
And who knows what alien bars
Will have been reached by your father's rock guitars
And after you and your friends have become men
Your father's legacy may be even more important then
And you will be there to receive that honor and respect
That in today's time too many choose rudely to neglect

Chorus

You are the son of the king
I can't wait to hear you sing
Right now crying is your thing
But you are the son of the king
You are the son of the king
You are the son of the king
I can't wait to hear you sing
One day you'll be the new king

The End

Please Don't Cut the Child

Obviously the way I feel about Michael should already say that I know he would never hurt a child. So you ask why write a poem that would suggest that he would? My answer is tabloid panic. It is also a cowardly way to complain. Again the thought of losing him takes precedence. When he did Thriller he was absolutely perfect. His color was perfect, his nose was perfect; the way he moved, sang and controlled the stage was perfect. Why would he have changed himself? It was another baffling thing for blacks to take in. But he did live near Hollywood and people there do strange things to themselves. Sometimes fans become critical of a change a star makes. The only thing I have ever wanted to change was my puffy eyes and I'm sure that wouldn't make me look less black. However as far as Michael is concerned I don't think he ever liked his nose and growing up under his father stressful hand made him a perfectionist. I guess he just kept trying to make it better. Of course Blacks saw it as a farther move from being us. So this poem is really not about whether Michael will do such a thing to his child rather it's about what he has done to himself. But he's a free man, intelligent and fully capable of making rational decisions; we didn't like it because it changed the image of what we wanted to see.

I have heard it said that a change on the outside doesn't change a person inside and I believe that but in Michael's case we are talking about a series of changes. In what a lot of blacks consider a deliberate move to alter himself to the point of not even resembling his ancestry. Those kinds of changes do change personality make up. Did Michael choose a white woman to bear his children so they would look more like him? You ask how can I engage this kind of conversation and still be a fan and still claim to love him. I am still a fan and I do still love him but

I am also me and I see what my mind sees. I haven't turned my
back on him but his intentions do puzzle me sometimes. Even
though you love somebody the why(s) don't go away because
you do. Michael is not just a big star he is the best that we have
and one always tries to protect the best that they have. You also
try to keep it the same.

03/6/97

I

Because I've lived so long
In the shadow of the throne
I'm afraid to say anything wrong
Because his kingdom must go on
I thought the king was strong
His judgment never wrong
I have followed every song
I have struggle to belong
While others went off to roam
I stayed firmly home
Living in my Michael zone
I've fought for the throne
Every time the enemy's drum
Came on with that storm
I was ageless like Strom
And when he had to perform
Against those trying to bring him down
I fought for his crown
Yes I've always been around
And I stood my ground
I knuckled myself down
And in that fox hole in the ground
I fired off my protest round
I have risked much for his crown

II

But this latest syndrome
That they say has come
Has made me feel like scum
I too like my king came from
The depth of the slum
And on that same drummer's drum
I have found freedom
I'm a part of the kingdom
But this plastic surgery syndrome
Is making me not know where he's coming from
And I swear I'm not dumb
And I'm not dropping the bomb
But how can I not succumb
To this strange talk that makes me feel numb
Little PJ when we were traded for rum
Brought here by force we didn't wanna come
I love your father and I would have risked my life
To save him although I didn't approve of his wife
But I realize he was in the midst of strife
But this thing he has for the surgeon's knife
I don't know you're his son but he doesn't look like you
Because of the cutting job he went through
And strange as it seems I don't know what he will do
Your mother can explain this better to you

III

Yes I may be very wrong
To question the throne
About some crazy unknown
But my doubts have grown
If his judgment is wrong

The issue becomes overwhelmingly strong
I fear what that could do to the throne
The throne may be overthrown
For black is black is black
A knife on the child is a knife in the back
I can't stand by if this is so I must attack
Michael if you are that much off track
It could only mean you hate the fact
That you were born black
But my heart can't and won't accept that
And I have no wish to attack
The kingdom that I love
That I've always tried to serve
That I have held above
Kept enemies from kicking it to the curve
For so long Michael we've only had you
As the one we listened and looked up to
And if this is something you've thought to do
Then you've fooled us and I feel sorry for you

Chorus

Please don't cut the child—the talk is driving me wild
Please don't cut the child—the talk is driving me wild
Please don't cut the child—the talk is driving me wild
Please don't cut the child—the talk is driving me wild

The End

Dedications

When your imagination about somebody has been as strong as mine about Michael has—it's easy to get your feelings mixed up, especially so when racial issues dominated you and escapism is a far journey not yet taken. When you are trying to reflect positive thoughts you have to keep repealing negative feelings. That's how it was when I thought of Michael, one moment I was praising him, the next I was questioning why he had did something that I couldn't approve of. But it wasn't Michael's prejudices I had to answer for; it was my own. How had I become so twisted inside that I would dare interpret his actions as my own, but I had, and I was still doing it. So when I became aware that I was doing that I would launch a counter-attack of appeasing verses. That was my way of apologizing, nevertheless, those initial expressions at the time they were written represented my true feelings, and I couldn't discard them.

Michael is so important to us that we all are mindful of attracting his displeasure. None of us can afford to insult him and God forbid that to occur. He has opened unheard of doors for us, giving us a range of opportunities up to now not even dreamed of. We are marveled that now our talents have become accepted around the world. Accepted because his unique talent and unwavering intelligence has turned the music world upside down. The respect for his accomplishments can't be wavered. Besides these things his moral and spirituality is so beautiful that I had to question anything I wrote that could contrast either. There are only two men in the United States I fear, one is the President and the other is Michael.

Never Forget My King Never Forget

02/20/97

I

In my heart I hurt and I care
But this ugliness is beating me I swear
I don't see clear victory for us anywhere
And I have this overpowering fear
I'm resentful but I'm aware
That my prejudices can hurt here
But my feelings are bare
Finally there's an heir
Whose mother is a typical White
Whose father appears that way by sight
But how will the child himself feel despite
Of his father's unseen appetite
Some say he wants to be white
But as certain as day is followed by night
With so many things wrong what can be right
Half-and-half will make the coffee light
How will the child feel about his skin
Being blacker than his parents have been?
Will he feel he's different then?
When will these feelings begin?
But more importantly when will they end?

II

Michael doesn't want to be a color he said
A thing not easily done I'm afraid
Especially when things happen in bed
You're black or white no matter what you think in your

head
And as long as the world treats people that way
I will be concerned about your feelings MJ
I get the same feelings when people holler you're gay
And like you I'm hoping for the day
When what Dr. King said fills the human heart okay
I ask you to overlook my concerns if they're wrong but
hey
It was just something I had to say
There are people trying not to be what they are
And you're such a tremendous star
I watch what I say—I dare not go too far
And I know what I think won't change who you are
But it may change things for little PJ and I know you love
him
But when he's around grandparents and not as white as
them
And when he's around the others and not as black well
here
The future is so unclear
It just causes me to fear
And I do fear as far as my understanding keeps me aware

III

Won't he think your being black
Had something to do with the level of this attack?
The one you suffered a short time back
If he does won't you appear pretty slack?
But I know you won't act
Like that famous running back
You've got to be real to change the way the facts will
impact
He has a lot to learn about being black
Now here I am casting this shadow and doubt
And probably don't know what I'm talking about

Making comments PJ can live without
But if you think it won't happen—what's your escape
  route?
Even though he's only a few weeks old
I hope his mother is an achieving soul
And will somehow in this take control
Which is a hard thing to do if she married for gold
But that's so unfair for me to say
I only know she's star stroke today
And people change with time okay
Yet and still regardless of that—happy father's day

Chorus

You're still the king and shall reign
Over your subjects domestic and foreign
Because you are the sovereign
My duty is to let you know you are
The one and only pop king star
But I'm afraid to go too far
Never forget who you are never forget
No matter how bad it gets you must not forfeit
The kingdom my king never forget
Never forget who you are never forget

The End

You're Still My King — My King

Undated

I

Of all that's been said and will be said
I realize now you're not afraid
The one thing you wanted most was a child
And now all I see is your smile
I see you've found that long desired peace
I no longer worry about the police
I know whatever error you've made
Will never again have that parade
In your life though I'd prepared myself for war
If they had been in real contention for your star
If they had hung you at the bar
If what they tried had gotten that far
I would've went to where you are
But thank God things didn't get that far
And you're still the superstar
Still shining brightly from afar
Maybe the picture you'll finally paint
Won't be that of a saint
But as this danger grows faint
And your image less taint
I'm grateful God kept you in charge
And kept your presence with me large
For you my king used your George
And you have defeated the mirage

II

You have proven yourself the man
And those who have a twisted stand
Can untwist if they can
And if they can't I'm still your fan
And you're still the man
The one and only real life Peter Pan
The one from Neverland
To your castle on French land
You're my favorite American
And your features though less African
Haven't stopped you from being a black man
Believe me my king I understand
One great star has called himself Carblinasian
Because he's half Asian
I know the old systems are aging
And you're still center staging
And as long as you're front-paging
You'll continue to be engaging
And as long as the storm is raging
It will make you more amazing
Your performances more dazzling
So keep on trail blazing
And let the buffaloes keep on glazing

III

They were treating you like a Benedict
And you never tried to be slick
They were making me sick
I'm glad it didn't result in armed conflict
So I won't have to show my courage
I can put my weapons back in storage
I won't have to cross that gorge
Because you're still in charge

You're still big and large
I can save my little George
I won't have to go on no warring voyage
Because you're in charge
I don't have to fear the enemy's mirage
So please stay big and large
I know things are changing all the time
I don't believe you committed a crime
So I'm putting it on the line
And I'm saying so with every rhyme
You're the king so what you do is fine
I believe you're of God's design
And evil has had its time
Tried but couldn't convict you of crime
Evil can kiss my behind
Along with those other fools in that line

IV

I wish you God's speed raising your child
I know he will have your profile
And have your pro style
And he won't grow up wild
He'll grow up like other princes and kings
And he'll be in charge of things
He'll know how and why the world swings
And why the Nightingale sings
And he won't fly blindly into things
And because he'll have his father's wings
He'll conquer many campaigns
I only hope I live to serve both reigns
And as you return to rule your world
I hope you'll be blessed with a little girl
That way there'll be a real Duchess of Earl
Who can swing and rock this world
And so I thank God for my time

And I thank him for my skill to rhyme
Because I'm using every line
Everywhere I go to raise the Michael sign
And I realize I shouldn't worship you
And that's not what I intended to do
You're always in my heart and view
I guess I've spent too much time loving you

Chorus

You're my king, my king and will always be of pop and
    swing
Unless you choose some other thing
You're still my king—my king and will always be of pop
    and swing
You're my king, my king and will always be of pop and
    swing
Unless you choose some other thing
You're still my king—my king and will always be of pop
    and Swing
Unless you choose some other thing

The End

Please Make Me Your First Knight

Undated

I

Michael, you're out of sight
But as a future friend I might
Wanna help you in this plight
So I'm asking you for the right
To be your first knight
As king you shouldn't have to fight
Enemies of the kingdom alone
Not when subjects are able and strong
I've trained so long
And I'm ready to get it on
All you got to do is phone
And say to me—get it on
And for the throne
I will come and I will come on strong

II

We were in trouble from day one
That's how the deal was done
That's how the slave trade was run
Now finally we have the gun
And I'm not threatening anyone
And like them I wanna have fun
But I'm not gon' stand by
And watch you on TV cry
I'm gon' do something about it
If that's amusement I can live without it
What they did was a form of apartheid
And even it has died

They showed such arrogance and pride
But we understand the evil they tried

III

Beyond making you the promise
That I'm not a doubting Thomas
I'll cut them down like pumice
Grinding away their numbers
I'll bust on them like the stealth bombers
Stop up the leaks like a gang of plumbers
I'll drive all traitors from among us
I know they wanna Vietcong us
I know this all sounds like a lot of bravado
But from here to Colorado
I'll be to them a desperado
You can bet on it in Los Vegas, Nevada
While you drink a Pina Colada
It's okay you can drink 'til you feel numb
You can drink 'til you bomb
We were traded for that rum
And if they would pay us we could all leave the slum

Chorus

Michael if you think I have done all right
Please make me your first knight
Michael if you think I have done all right
Please make me your first knight
Michael if you think I have done all right
Please make me your first knight and let me fight
I want to make everything right
Please make me your first knight—my knight

The End

Michael You're My Song

Undated

I

When you were just a lad
Long before "I'm Bad"
I spent hours at my pad
Listening and I might add
You were captivating even then
But now that we both are men
Grown up both outward and in
Loving you has always been
A real treat for me my friend
And I hope our friendship will never end
Your music I have absolved
Successfully and evolved
With it many problems I have solved
Spiritually we are involved
And no one can take that from me
In my spirit you will always be
An energy that helps me
In my soul—you have that ability
I'm sorry if I'm out of control
But I feel so deep in my soul
Sometimes you're its daily goal
Forgive me if I'm too bold
I should know better and I'm much too old
But if we lose you the world would be cold

II

Some would say my feelings are unhealthy
That I will never see you because you're too wealthy
And maybe they know but they can't tell me
Because I'm committed as long as I am free
As long as I'm above the shadows of the grave
This is the way I choose to behave
This is what God giving you gave
My choice is to be free and like you be nobody's slave
I may be wrong but I believe the things you do can save
So asked when I will leave you I say nave
I have courage but I am not entirely brave
My prince I dare not bore you but I'm your music slave
I soar through your music 'til I get myself high
I would be Billy Gene if I were not a guy
But don't worry I'm as straight as any arrow can fly
But that doesn't stop this metaphysical thing between you
    and I
The worse thing ever was seeing you on TV cry
If anything happened to you inside I would die
People were talking about your suicide over that awful lie
And all I could think if that happened how would I get by
What would I do if I knew you would never sing again
That you would never again perform and make my world
    spin?
It was too awful for me even too pretend
Oh I would live on but it would be without my greatest
    friend

III

My wife doesn't know about this thing between us
And I'm afraid to tell her cause it could demean us
I don't want to explain the secrecy between us
I've worked too hard and long to gain her trust

No man should worship another the way I do you
When I know that you are only human too
And so for many years I have done this thing I do
I only hope that what I've said is and will come true
I hate to think that any of this will offend you
If so I apologize but I'm doing what I feel I have to do
You are a performer and I know you understand
Sometimes fantasy can appeal when nothing else can
I would guess that is why you bought Neverland
And maybe why so many think you're the Pan
Singing the way you do I'm helplessly your fan
I have followed you over air, sea and land
I know you've had some trouble and I think you came out
    of it well
As well as anyone could when faced with so much hell
Maybe that's why to me you are more of a fairy tale
A frog to a prince come true and I hope you never fail
To entertain us the way only you can do
My strength and armor and honor I offer to protect you
In ending I dedicate in part this undertaking to you and
    your son too
My principles are ancient but they have always brought me
    through

Chorus

Michael—you're my song and you're my cup of tea
You've done so much in your life that pleases me
I hope by saying this, my words will help keep you free
From all curses that they would and do cast on thee
Michael—you're my song and you're my cup of tea
Michael—you're my song and you're my cup of tea

The End

By Right of Succession

After the trouble and the marriage to Lisa Marie ended, Michael disappeared. He remarried again and his reclusive ways returned. He hooked up with a Saudi prince and rumor had it—started to build amusement parks. His pop kingdom for a long time, my home was fading away. Rather than let it drift off into oblivion, I wrote this chapter, hoping to salvage the dream he had—that he seemed to have abandoned. But I still hoped he would return.

It had become obvious that we had to start looking for someone else to lead. Perhaps the hurt had been too much, I didn't know I couldn't find much information it although I was sure it was out there but I hadn't taken the time to look. He wasn't communicating through the media and I couldn't blame him, the way it had tried to do him. Still in his world you can't prosper without the media. How long could he avoid using it? Having gone so long without word of his return I had become desperate, something had to break or we had to find a substitute. I had listened to each CD now many times let's say hundreds of times and I wanted something new. Where was Michael? When was he coming back? I talked to family but I never let them know how upset I was. They were not big fans of Michael and probably wouldn't have understood the stress I was feeling. My nightmare went on and my need to know one way the other increased. Was he coming back or wasn't he?

Diva You Must Bring Our World Back

Undated

I

The number to beat was 61
They said it couldn't be done
Sammy swung in the sun
But Mark would be the one
And when he did it the crowd screamed
And baseball was redeemed
Still to me it seemed
Those things I had dreamed
Hoped for wasn't gon' come
The confusion in the kingdom
Still centered around freedom
It was where we were from
Most times I was alone
But with the king gone
I bought ticket for her show
Where he was I didn't know
I had no choice I had to go
We were hurting you know
But could I convince her to be queen?
You know whom I mean
The one with the Velvet Rope routine
The other Jackson dancing machine
Her forces could sweep the planet
All I would have to say is rule it Janet
Take us to the next level
The devil with the devil
This time you can take it all
The umpire yelled play ball

But I was thinking about Inaugurate Hall
In the wind were signs of early fall
And London still had Paul
And Berlin had taken down the wall

II

Many years must pass
Before young PJ has the brass
To go before his father and ask
If he can take over the task
Using common sense
His father at great expense
Avoided the pretense
Of having to convince
A jury of his innocence
His money became his defense
And though the pressure was immense
He used it and jumped that fence
At that time I was writing part time
Working for those who punished crime
I did my forty hours but no overtime
The rest of my time was spent on rhyme
The king hadn't performed in 4 years
Giving reasons to my fears
I missed all the cheers
Remembering his tears
I was beginning to believe he wouldn't come back
It had been a long time since I had seen his act
Couldn't I now accept the fact?
He was more white than black
At Motown he was his team's quarterback
But he had been left that track
Boys to Men was the new contact
The biggest group Motown had on contract
The Jackson Five were gone

The Supremes—a yesterday song
Smoky was the only one still carrying on
From the old days and Smoky still was strong

III

As I waited on a comeback sign
Questions came to mind
Is she pretty? Yes she's very fine
She had black skin and it shined
Her lips were like deep red wine
She sent fire up and down my spine
You see she's the kind
That blows your mind
How I really felt I couldn't define
Your know love makes you blind
I was looking forward to her concert
The newspapers were full of dirt
The nation had suffered a great hurt
And it was all about Monica's skirt
The dress she kept had trapped the President
A lot of unnecessary money would be spent
Hello, the President is not here
But I guess what's fair is fair
The question is do you really care?
Do you know why they're polluting the air?
I'll tell you they wanna win in two thousand—don't they?
And they'll do anything to accomplish that—won't they?
But for us the true colors of the dollar
Is in blood and no white collar
Up there is interested in helping the hood
Other than that it's all good
If you understood
Let's make it good
Step to the curve
It don't take nerve

So don't perturb
The Diva is the queen if she will serve

IV

He was a record breaker
As big as an LA Laker
He fought the Undertaker
Ventura was no faker
A big redneck Quaker
But in California owning an acre
Is something you doubt
Something you dream about
But I'm not gon' pout
The queen is in route
Her brother the king
Came up short on the thing
The queen will sing
She will make us swing
That old familiar saying
Is "I'm not playing"
What's the use of obeying?
The kingdom is decaying
The king has abandoned us
So whom can we trust?
How can we escape our disgust?
The nation is in rust
The nation is in us
We're not at the back of the bus
We're trying to hold this space
If the queen won't take her place
Who will we put in her space?
Get that knife out my face
If I'm ugly that's okay that's fine
It ain't your face it's mine
Like I said its party time
Give me the rhythm and rhyme

V

We need to rekindle our belief
We must have a new war chief
His promise will not end our grief
His word to return not bring relief
We have been waiting
And it's so irritating
Every day anticipating
Why is he hesitating?
Why doesn't he come back?
Is he afraid of being black?
Will we not watch his back?
They're not gon' attack
We only have the Diva now
Maybe he will reappear in Moscow
The cops failed they didn't make him bow
There is nothing they can do about it now
I saw her Velvet Rope tour
And still I'm not really sure
That she will be the cure
The king has to stop acting immature
He has to face the tragedy
Or give up the monarchy
He can't be the majesty
If he's afraid to face history
Diva the kingdom is yours
Reluctantly I had chose
This beautiful black rose
It will be hard but she can reopen the doors
She doesn't have to defend her right to be
We've lost so many gains in history
So many hard fought losses we need a victory
She's the only one who can save this fantasy

Chorus

Diva—you must bring our pop world back
Promise us you will stay black
We lost the king in an attack
Our people will be lost if we don't get back
There is no excuse for that
Here is where the king sat
Diva—you must bring our pop world back
We believe you can do that
Diva—you must bring our pop world back
Diva—you must bring our pop world back

The End

I Just Wanted To Tell You These Things Little PJ

Undated

I

First little PJ as a knight I'm sworn
Been that way since before you were born
I spend a lot of time on the phone
Just to find out what's been going on
People been saying behind closed doors
That one day the kingdom will be yours
But if your dad don't return
You'll have bridges to burn
Books of music to learn
The kingship is something you got to earn
You'll have the adulation of fans
They'll stand with raised hands
And will do so across many lands
They'll be like your father's fans
But by then that would've been long ago
You're just a baby I know
You've got along way to go
Before you do your first show
But I'll be watching you grow
He loves you greatly—yes I know
A thousand of times he's said so
You give his face such a glow
He might not want you to do his thing
He might not want you to be the king
He might not want you to rule the land of swing
He might not want you wear this ring
He might not want you burdened with the crown

His world was almost torn down
To protect you—he's raising you in a small town
The pressure hasn't been around
You will have a normal childhood
I know that makes him feel good
His hope is that you won't be misunderstood
All of his life, he has tried to do good
Right now he's doing things for the hood
His theme parks will bring jobs and that is good

II

I'm just saying these things so you'll be ready
Your responsibilities will be heavy
You won't be racing in your Chevy
Your personal driver will be the one at the levy
Instead you'll grow up like Prince Charles' boys
You'll have all kinds of incredible toys
Your friends will be your daddy's choice
In that you have no voice
He's going to protect you child
You're not gon' get caught up in something wild
Get punished the way he did—not you child
He'll control your life style
His father did that for him
But it won't be the same way as it was with them
He wondered if his daddy loved him
Joe kept a lot of pressure on them
But Joe was trying to make them great
He couldn't allow or afford a mistake
He got them ready for their big break
Motown came in the picture and didn't hesitate
It changed their world and everything
It was the break that would eventually made your father
    king
Go visit your Grandparents—it'll be a good thing

In their yard they have swings and you can swing
I heard Grandfather Joe's been ill
But he's a man of incredible will
Even if he is sick with you there he won't be still
There are many things he may feel
He has to say that he didn't say to your dad
I hate that he feels so bad
He saw you through like a good dad
A little hard but in many ways he wasn't bad
He was just too strict
But his actions didn't contradict
They turned into hit after hit
He lifted his family out of their poverty pit

III

How many times I got to tell those asking
Little PJ I know time is passing
They're worried about the kingdom lasting
But nothing could be worse than over tasking
A young boy likes you PJ to me
I tell them his father ain't gon' let that be
He's aware of his responsibility
He's got to be a father first don't they see
They expect too much of him
He's human I keep telling them
Now when your aunt came out of the gym
And she is beautiful; she is smart and trim
I said he might not wanna go back to that
He might not wanna bring back his act
It's not like pulling rabbits out of a hat
He's enjoying being an aristocrat
He didn't steal his money from the poor
He's been on the other side of that door
He knows when you have nothing you can't score
For those in poverty he wants to do more

But it's gon' take a lot more time
And it's hard when you've been accused of a crime
Whoever said the light was always lime
Sometimes you crawl through the slime
You have to get down on your belly
And snake through the filth and jelly
It takes that to be a Michael J or an R Kelly
You feel like saying woo Nellie
I wanna get off this ride
Your father worried so and he almost died
You see when your hurt's deep inside
It's hard getting over wounded pride
Especially when you feel you've done nothing wrong
Nothing more than sing your song
Suddenly you're threatened and freedom's near gone
I thank God that they couldn't take his throne

Bridge

I just wanted to tell you these things little PJ
They may not be things your father would say
Problems unsolved can comeback on you one day
They can be revisited upon your child they say
I just wanted to tell you these things little PJ
I just wanted to tell you these things little PJ
I just wanted to tell you these things little PJ
Because there are things your father won't say

The End

Monarch of Pop

Undated

I

Needing to fill a hole in my soul
I went back to Control
Rhythm Nations not then old
Forced me to behold
If the king was in France
And he will not dance
The kingdom is a dying romance
If he doesn't come from France
We don't stand a chance
Evil will advance
The last show was in Moscow
He has two children now
As sweat from my brow
Fell I thought I don't know now
I wanna save my world
I want the Rhythm Nation's girl
But I was no Duke of Earl
I couldn't sing nor rock the world
But as I wrote these lines
Reading tomorrow's signs
Hoping to open minds
To put light behind the blinds
It's a matter of circumstance
She could lead this advance
She could give us back the dance
Without it we don't stand a chance
We will be gone in a glance
While the king is in France

I didn't wanna profile
But since he's in exile
Or someplace on the Nile
I'm saying it—I like the Diva's smile

II

I want to ask somebody right here
And I want your answer to be clear
Have you seen the Diva this year?
Did the people cheer?
Did she make 'em care?
Did she represent herself there?
For the music we'd go anywhere
So is this the Diva's year
Can she assume power?
Deliver us at the midnight hour?
I fear that I may cower
Because we have nothing but our
Belief in the king
Without him doing his thing
What will happen to Swing?
The Diva has to sing
So we can choose
Her rock, pop, rhythm and blues
Someone to fill the king's shoes
These are my views
If he continues to refuse
The throne will become old news
We have paid our dues
And we have the right to choose
I know we all love the king
But if he's not gon' sing
Not gon' do his thing
Then the Diva should replace the king
There is no other solution

It's in the constitution
To avoid a revolution
Brothers we must make the substitution

III

Most of us feel the same way
With two children no one calls him gay
He could come back today
Unless he wants to give the throne away
Maybe he has simply stepped down
If so she deserves the crown
And that feeling is going around
If he has given up this ground
And is living someplace else large?
Have we become a mirage?
We need someone to take charge
The Diva's got the George
She has made it over the years
I respect the king's tears
But I have my own fears
And we need the cheers
From places like Central Park
We must choose a new monarch
To lead us from this dark
Her music will kindle that spark
Dying in our hearts
We support the arts
We play our roles and do our parts
But we can't keep throwing darts
Looking for restarts
The kingdom once ruled the charts
Our leader was Number One
Now we don't even have a top gun
How many times can we hit and run?
How long can that kind of thing be fun?

How long can we hide from the sun?
Perhaps the king's work is done

Bridge

When you see her tonight
She is his sister and by right
Under the spotlight
If you call yourself a knight
You must do what's right
We must appoint her tonight
We didn't make the king stop
We need a monarch of pop

The End

Marie Could Have Never Been Queen

Undated

I

We're not gon' perish cause the king won't do his routine
We have no choice but elect the Diva queen
I agree the king might've had a dream
But Marie no matter the effort will never be a Supreme
You got to have a chocolate or Madonna soul
Or what Janet had in Control
Though Marie's rich and bold
She would have never made it to solid gold
The king was hurt and easy to infatuate
He recognized the problem with her too late
I don't know what it cost his estate
What do you pay for an error in fate?
I don't know what she wanted to gain
For helping him over his pain
For giving him shelter from the rain
For altering the pressure in his brain
So why didn't he help her with her CD?
Was he afraid she wouldn't be
Like his lovely friend ET?
After all Elvis was Marie's daddy
How did she make Michael so unhappy?
I don't wanna sound tacky
But was she like her pappy
Or maybe she was too daffy
She was nothing like Katy
Katy is a real special lady
Marie would've been better off with a Baity
You know what I'm saying baby

The girl belongs to a Dick Tracy
When Michael took her shopping at Macy
He would've been better off taking Sadie
He would've known she was a street lady

II

I really can't blame Marie
For choosing his company
For seeing a chance to be
Someone in world history
She went for it you know
I don't know why he said no
Did she want to be in his show?
She didn't care about him being a Negro
But a woman like that can use you up
Drank you dry and drain your cup
No matter what you do you never equal up
She'll be the big dog and you'll be the pup
Your act would become her act
With somebody pulling on you like that
Creating fear you won't comeback
After all he had suffer a vicious attack
He needed time to recover
He didn't need a pushy lover
He probably heard that from his mother
And Jermaine his brother
At least that is what I believe
The girl was a rich little tease
And she was told to leave
He might've said mother please
But Katherine doesn't play
Around when it comes to MJ
Janet probably said mama okay
If you and daddy feel that way
When he collapsed Katy went to his bed

And Mrs. Katy probably said
Michael: Get it in your thick head
This woman makes me afraid

III

Now the newest and latest wife
I think won't interfere with his life
And she won't cause strife
Won't back stab him with a knife
She thinks he's the greatest ever
And they'll probably stay together
The one thing she is—is clever
She'll be there in stormy weather
Would LM have done that—I say no
You don't have to if you're a rich ho
I haven't got that itch
I didn't call her a bitch
But a nasty little witch
Anyway life is a bitch
You know what I mean
I'd never say that about a sleep in queen
It wouldn't be good
For the knighthood
And the king has always stood
For good in the knighthood
We know how to talk
We know how to walk
We believe in the light
We believe in his might
He could ban me from being a knight
So I would never say something out of spite
Other people say she's shady
I got nothing against the lady
Only that when he was sick
She hit him hard and quick

Maybe that's the way they politic
Maybe that's love in that Beverly Hill's click

Bridge

Marie could have never been the pop queen
She couldn't master the routine
Just like Charles in England
She never had what it took to rule Swingland
Michael's kingdom is not like that in England
Neither Marie nor Charles could survive gangland
Charles lost Princess Di and yes we have seen
Marie could have never been the pop queen

The End

By Right of Succession

9/3/98

I

When Hurricane Earl
Was sweeping my world
I saw you girl
Behold the black pearl
Heir to the throne
A lady of song
In this world of wrong
Still turning on
Hearts that have grown
Cold as stone
The world is unkind
Yet you came into mine
At last a star did shine
And you're so fine
And it's show time
It's your time to shine
Across that stage
It's still a Jackson age
As you engage
The end of the decade
Your heart will be obeyed
For we have paid
And we celebrate
You as queen of the new pop age
Beautiful and stately
Asking, "What have you done for me lately?"
But I fear greatly
Not knowing what awaits me

I'm afraid for the king
His was a noteworthy campaign
I loved being under his reign
But he has given me no new songs to sing

II

There were thousands on hand
Each one a potential fan
Having been rocked by your band
Believing in this land
The low can rise and be the mighty
Nothing taken lightly
You did excite me
And I wanted you to invite me
That night to crown you queen
Like those in your routine
I was a part of the scene
Out there trying to scream
Your name as the supreme
Ruler in the pop world—a dream
I believe you will redeem
And I will serve you my queen
I believe the king will not return
Never again will I see him burn
With that for which I yearn
I spend the money I earn
Freely given for your song
Perhaps I am wrong
But if he won't reclaim the throne
Refuses to turn us on
His right as king is gone
And you are so strong in song
By right and blood heir to the throne
I mean if he is really gone
I must obey my heart

Broken and torn apart
In his absence I beg you to start
Rebuilding this broken heart

III

I am not betraying my king
But if he won't reign
And seeing you do your thing
It seems a hopeless campaign
To remain loyal to the king
We need someone to reign
I feel estranged
But things have changed
I wanna go back
But I question if he's black
And they attack
Successful males who are black
If that's holding him back
I can respect that
But it doesn't change the fact
He's got to get back on track
If he's testing combat with you
Seeing what the enemy will do
Then he's wronging you
And that with me will never do
Some say he's not black
And never coming back
He fears a media attack
And he fears being called black
But his music is black
Even if it has a rock format
There's nothing wrong with that
But to me he'll always be black
Like him I hate color lines
But that doesn't change the times

We can't live behind blinds
We got to live where the light shines

Chorus

We once only served him
But we by popular election
And by right of succession
Make you queen of the realm
We still and will love him
But we want to rule the realm
So we chose you by election
And by right of succession

The End

The King Is Gone — Long Reign The Queen

Undated

I

In typical Jackson style
You performed while
In the balcony I looked on
Thinking how suited you were for the throne
Since your brother's gone
But it's not my decision alone
Yes we want him back
But what can we do about that
What can we change to ease his fear of attack?
I don't pretend to wear that hat
I can't council him on that
So in the balcony I sat
Estranged and unable to forget
My king as you did your set
You were so petite
So sexy and sweet
Obviously you're neat
Lightning on your feet
I watched and you didn't make
That night a mistake
I thought my heart would break
But it didn't even ache
Had I found my queen?
From what I seen
You were clean and mean
But would you be our queen?
How many had seen your routine?
Your face on that magazine

Marie must've been turning green
She wanted so badly to be the queen
She may have shared the king's address
But she wasn't you my princess
She lacked that Jackson finesse
Though her father one time was the best
The king of rock and roll no less
And he did lead the west
But that was a long time ago
Things have changed even though
He took a lot from the Negro
He never acknowledge that he did so
So I don't think I'm cheating her
I just can't see me needing her
I can't see myself greeting her
I was glad when I heard he was leaving her

II

I watched you from start to finish
Your energy didn't diminish
You must be hell at tennis
Like Popeye you are your spinach
How could any Diva compete against you?
You did what the Jacksons do
Your blood is true blue
That night all eyes were on you
As the tempo of your show grew
I guess like others I knew
After him the throne belonged to you
No one else for me will do
I fell under your spell and I did agree
There's no one else we need see
Right now if I had the key
And the power I would decree
And give you the monarchy

Maybe it's time we set your brother free
It's time we let him raise his family
I know there are some who disagree
But he's been through hell
It's time to ring the bell
It's time we let that boat sail
It's time we accept his farewell
He's been a good king and for us done well
He can't give his whole life to our fairy tale
Can't always be our nightingale
And I know he loves us but well
We have got to let him go
We got to do the right thing you know
We got to let him go
Why kill a hero?
I think it's your time
You're in your prime
And you're so damn fine
I wish you were mine
Any man would have you if he could
You look that good
And you're doing good for the hood
And you're not misunderstood
You have the General in your camp
And he's nobody's scamp
He's extremely high amp
He's much brighter than any other lamp

III

You got everything going for you my lady
Millions of fans who are crazy
For you and no one can say you're lazy
You continually amaze me
I don't know how large your following has to be
Your brother had that charisma you see

I don't know if anyone has his specialty
Understand he built this fantasy
But if anybody else can do it—it's you—you see
You should be the sovereignty
Since the kingdom exist
And you're top of the list
I think you can do this
You can fill the abyss
You're in great condition
And we're in transition
If God has chosen you for this mission
All you need is ambition
You don't need anybody's permission
I'm a knight of tradition
I must serve the monarch
I will not protest nor march
I will let no one scorch
The ground on which you stand if you hold the torch
You could blaze a new trail
Lead many to freedom as well
As well as strengthen the black male
So my lady lift up your sail
And pitch it in the wind
May our friendship never end?
Like your brother I want to be your friend
Forever with you I'll ride the wind
We have heard enough of the notes
Our dollars will cast our votes
If you will learn the sovereign ropes
That would fulfill many hopes
I don't want the royal bloodline broken
We don't need another token
Like Marie too outspoken
We need a healer -- our wounds are open
You could do that for us
You could have our trust
You could quench this thirst
If you would become our first

Chorus

By right of succession
It is our right to change a selection
To convene a free market election
If we need direction
If we need protection
If there's indiscretion
We're entitle to make a correction
By right of succession
The king is gone—long reign the queen
The king is gone—long reign the queen

The End

We Got To Know Brother Cause We're Covert Undercover

Undated

I

You know I don't know what you can afford
But since the settlement you haven't sung a chord
As far as I know you haven't even try to record
So quite naturally I'm abhorred
As a knight I must carry my sword
And like the highlander I've given my word
Some heads will roll
If the truth is told
They can't imprison your soul
They don't have that control
You've got more platinum and gold
Than I will ever behold
Is it possible that you agreed
To give the devil such a lead
That heaven itself would bleed?
I know that's a horrid read
Does God intend that we not succeed?
Because our Adam turned white from his black seed
And has undoubtedly abandoned an important race
Relegating heaven to second place
Do the dark forces block the chase?
Why are the forces of good down on our case?
How can we get back on base?
I hate to think but if this is the case
We can't take another slap in the face
When we're trying so hard to have yesterday's erased
Men fall in love with what they like

And you have had a life long affair with the mike
To suddenly tell music to take a hike
Walk off and leave it like Tina left Ike
That's not a nail through the hand that's a spike
Some of us miss the rabbit on the bike

II

Every day I look into the depths of my heart
Wondering how you withstood yours torn apart
Years ago there was Randy Record March
Radio was not much more than a voltage arch
And nothing stayed pressed unless it had starch
To think I will never again hear my pop monarch
Is like seeing that black effigy hanging in the park
No agreement for us could be more dark
It would condemn the last spark
Of the hope we have of ever finding the new ark
Seeing the rain clouds gather with the approaching dark
Wondering not if but when will you make your mark
Your return Michael to us is mandatory
You were taken at the height of your glory
For waiting fans yours was a classic horror story
That belongs in the ancient Greek category
More unsettling than scenes from "Glory"
Reminisce of Roots and Haley's Tobee
And I shiver in my boots
Lord not another Roots
Must we eat only bitter fruits?
Suddenly a spike shoots
Up my spine and it recruits
That which constitutes
Fears so deeply embedded they seem unlearned
Of black bodies castrated, beaten and burned
Thoughts of human decency overturned
The brutality we received we never earned

Crosses burning and secret orders
In memberships killing for racial borders
Things to vile to be seen on today's video recorders
Why are we still waiting on heaven for marching orders?

III

Our people are too fragmented to believe in anything
We were never expected to have a king after Dr. King
Except some white democrat elected on a string
Hanging in back of black minds—yet swing
Has given us hope while we're losing the ring
With drugs in our blood we worry about the FBI sting
The simple things God gave us we have lost
Careless misfortunes every day drive up the cost
We get to the top and find we're still not the boss
We brush our teeth but we forget to floss
Freedom for some of us is completely lost
In prison they talk about a salad toss
I know his politics were never a hidden thing
He was simply a singing king
Sent in this world to show us how to swing
Lord knows he did his thing
But of all people he knew things would not stay the same
So I don't understand this running game
Soon his time too will be gone
I have to wonder because he hasn't been on
No one can reach him by phone
When I call him he's gone
He's almost never home
Some say he's moved near Rome
I can't prove them wrong
So presently my song
Is to ask him to make what he feels known
Before the kingdom is overgrown
All the rumors have shown

It could wind up overthrown
We need someone to turn us on
Michael please comeback—the kingdom is almost gone

Chorus

We got to know brother because we have to know what we
    have to cover—will Janet take over?
We got to know brother because we have to know what we
    have to cover—will Janet take over?
Right now no one is above him and we still serve the one
    glove
But push has come to shove—Do we have a pigeon or a
    dove?
We got to know brother because we have to know what we
    have to cover—will Janet take over?
We got to know brother because we have to know what we
    have to cover—will Janet take over?
We got to know my brother because we're covert
    undercover
We got to know my brother because we're covert
    undercover

The End

Thank You God

I was grateful for the miracle that had befallen us. Michael was back. He had survived. Though things had changed he was still a mighty presence for good in the world. I had been at this enterprise seven years, and though others doubted, I knew he would be back. Seeing him perform lifted me from the September Eleventh depression that seemed to have swallowed up the whole world. We had been attacked on home soil, and it wasn't metaphysically, it was real. The day the towers fell changed the landscape of American lives. Suddenly our whole world had changed from addressing imaginary enemies to addressing real ones. Some had portrayed Michael as some kind of fiend, but now they had witnessed real evil. It wasn't a story the media had to grow. Bin Laden was a real villain who orchestrated the murder of thousands of Americans. For seven years Michael had been out of sight but he was back. There had been doubt that he would return but somehow I knew he would and I was very glad he had.

Before we got to see him we were hit by a monstrous act, the nine-eleven terror attack. I would spend a lot of time thinking about that. I was on the last or next to the last chapter and there wasn't much more to say. I had covered everything I wanted to cover but this attack open my eyes in new ways. I had thoughts that I hadn't thought since Vietnam. I had seen a racial divide coming made highly evident by the OJ Simpson first trial verdict but suddenly all of that was gone. Suddenly we were forced to recognize that we all were Americans. We wanted the same kinds of things. We enjoyed the same foods. We went to the same places and bet on the same things. We couldn't afford our indifference anymore. Being black wasn't as important as being American first. This one incident would heal racial divides for a long time.

So I Thank You God

Undated

I

Though saddened by a deadly score
I am more grateful than before
Never thought I'd see him anymore
After nineteen ninety four
No I'm not kidding you
I didn't know what I was going to do
I might've thought it too
Saying Michael who?
Heterosexual I had other issues to raise
I don't know gays or people wit' strange ways
Though it took over two thousand days
For him to get back in phase
He was still special to me
Still the one I wanted to see
His debacle wasn't funny
Lucky he had that monster money
Though the media tried to confuse
And the N word was seldom used
It was like he was wearing Simpson's shoes
Remember how they made the News
And in a backward flash
I remembered Johnny talking trash
I didn't want to be rash
And I don't smoke hash
But OJ was lucky he didn't get the lash
But he had that cash
And cash ran the hundred-meter dash
It was the money that set him free

And that bugged people like me
We didn't have that kind of money see
It's a screwed up democracy
And with money still
Freedom is the dollar bill
Only money stops overkill
We may never heal
So pop another pill
And try to keep it real
After all we know the deal
Only God has free will

II

Look he made it to the top
And he didn't stop
'Til he became the King of Pop
Sometimes I hate a cop
If he's doing what I think he's doing
I believe I'm worth knowing
I heard that sucker blowing
And it's cold but my words are flowing
And I wondered how could a guy that rich
Get hit on like a bitch
He didn't even see the personality switch
That kind of trust makes me itch
I believe what's dead belongs under the ground
Knowing most of the time the truth can be found
But you can't mess around
You have to be ready when it's time to get down
Make the statement if it's true
It took two trials but they got OJ too
Don't think that they can't get you?
In this case they had nothing so they withdrew
And now another century is here
Again we have come to cheer

I wonder does he still have that fear
And will his name ever clear
Fading off track
I decided to go back
To being black
It's not an invisible fact
Things change when you're black
It took a long time for him to come back
And still have that impact
We will go anywhere to see his act
He's like the milk in Mother Nature's breast
And we suck without protest
Still that was one hell of a mess
Twin Towers falling in the west
I remember Bucharest
He was at his best
And two wars less
Osama bin Laden won't confess
But he can't live under this sun
Look at the murders he has done
And I'm still praying to the One
To one ancient God and his son

III

I have learned to be particular
But his shows were always spectacular
After all the man is a superstar
He fought and won his war
And he's back making cabbage
As always he's beyond average
And what I was seeing wasn't a mirage
He must've spent a lot of George
But he's always had that flair
And always had that dare
The miracle and the scare

Afterward he's made us care
For seven years I stood my ground
Like a prisoner I was bound
While everything else went down
I waited on his sound
I knew he'd be back around
In him I had found
Jackie Wilson and James Brown
Coming from a small town
Captured I believed
When he returned I'd receive
I just couldn't leave
My love for him was retrieved
When he became free
Not innocent or guilty
Though the situation was filthy
I believed he would sing to me
I'm not afraid to look back
Because we both are black
He's finally beyond attack
He's got a new soundtrack
I've wanted it since he announced it
What I've heard I've bounced it
In my head and I know it's a hit
All those days I sit
Fingers on the keyboard
Like it was a sword
Every thought and word
I used and when I was bored
Thinking of him lifted me
I knew he had a family
He had kids just like me
So I waited for him on TV

IV

I've been faithful so long
I forgot about right and wrong
I just wanted to be strong
Strong enough to sing every song
Every song he ever made
A warrior in the trade
I sharpened my blade
For battle and I didn't fade
His struggle was real to me
It filled me with memory
Going back to 93
The last year he was free
But along with the tragedy
Came the strategy
For me to be a knight
So I've trained to fight
I too felt the fright
Missed him most at night
I worried about his absentee
When I felt that misery
Everything that he
Suffered—happened to me
I took it personally
I was lost in the same infinity
But I didn't lose my sanity
There was no hell in me
The kingdom was all I had
I kept on praying saying: "I'm bad"
And though I was sad
I was hardly ever mad
At him for leaving me
I knew he had to be free
Seven years of history
Passed before I would see

Him again on stage
Still I remember the rage
The stories on front page
How he'd lost his age
I wanted him to comeback
I wanted him to be black
I wanted him to forget the attack
I wanted him to be the Mack
The way he was back then
I hadn't seen him but I did pretend
Even as I faced my own sin
I believed we were honorable men

V

You think I'm a crazy fan
But I'm an average man
Doing everything I can
To uphold this great land
Yes I've been lost in this fantasy
That's the only thing he left me
But I've pressed on 'til I could see
The day he'd return and set me free
I've had some hard times
But I kept on with my lines
Watching for the signs
I wrote many rhymes
Waiting for his return
My loyalty he had earned
And I have learned
It takes a slow burn
If you don't wanna burn out
The one thing I don't doubt
Is everyone gets talked about
That's the human route
But seven years was enough

Lord knows it's been rough
But I had the right stuff
And I didn't fall for the bluff
I kept my heart and mind serious
It's not that it's mysterious
He was important to me
I'm glad that he's free
Many times I've thought
Of the fight that would've been fought
If a guilty verdict had been brought
Thank God that appeal won't be sought
Those times for me were tender
The things I remember
Made the darkest September
Thank God Michael didn't surrender
Luckily no permanent hurt was done
I didn't have to hurt anyone
And once again in Katherine's son
A victory would be won
We've been down so long
To see him comeback so strong
In top form on every song
And that make me glad that I held on

VI

How many years it's been seven
And God knows up in Heaven
That September eleven
Didn't bring us the lucky seven
But the heat is coming on
Our prayers are strong
We will avenge this wrong
I was setting at work that day alone
When I heard the city had gotten blown up
Those murdering bastards had shown up

Put our whole nation on hold up
But now that that control's up
They've got nothing to be happy about
I know us and I know we will reroute
And take those Asses out
Not long before Michael danced and shout
I remember those moments of happiness
Though now we will have that less
Because of Bin Laden's craziness
In NYC and DC we're putting people to rest
And we still have a lot to learn
Innocent victims there did burn
To an awful death they did not earn
Still I was happy for Michael's return
I believe I can make it now
No matter what I can take it now
I know somehow
Evil one day will bow
We can leave it behind
We can be one in mind
Damn those who are blind
It's a cruel world and we have to be more kind
But this first tragedy we have got to go through
Afterward God may show us a different view
Until then to each other we have to be true
I know that for each other our love is overdue
But when people start to murder in God's name
And not be seen as criminally insane
Then the world is in for a lot of pain
Even now life here will never be the same
Now that an airplane
Has been used as a bomb by these insane
Murderers who proclaim
It in Allah's name
No matter what people tell you
This is only something evil would do
But still I'm grateful God that you

Allowed Michael to break back through
So he can once again lift his cause
But right now we have to pause
Because there are too many seesaws
Too many people breaking your laws

VII

After the thing with the President
And Michael I spent
A lot of time at my resident
And I don't want to misrepresent
I know there's good in my kind
But this new thing was hard on my mind
The world seemed blind
Obviously its values weren't well defined
This was the deepest under I've ever been
I was slam up against sin
Against forces so strong I can't pretend
To have thought Good would win
But like my king I knew
That God would be true
That we would come through
We will do what we have to do
And through that dark course
We will find the force
We will overcome our remorse
Because in America God is still the source
He has always lifted me
He made it possible for me to see
The greatness in humanity
Even though there is insanity
All over running around
But tonight I'm gon' get down
The kingdom has found
The one that wore the crown

Now that he's back may he stay forever?
May he bring us together?
And though evil is clever
I believe it will never
Overcome the goodness I see
Only through goodness we will be free
Thank God we have liberty
In this country everyone is free
And like Michael let's give
To the world in which we live
Now my heart lit up after he arrived
I thanked God that he had survived
Though I don't have much
Through those long dark times of the search
I believed God sent Michael and staying in touch
I took his and my problems to church

VIII

Things haven't grown cheaper
Spiritually we'd grown weaker
But I am my brother's keeper
It doesn't take a heat seeker
To threaten me — I think I know
We still have a long way to go
I'm afraid because I'm a Negro
And I saw Michael's woe
How it kept him from the show
The distant we have got to row
In light of that is not short
But the empire is not mine to abort
I've looked at every thought
And I've honored the way he fought
Sometimes you win and it isn't clear
All the time I've been here
He was someplace out there

I cared so I kept an ear
Opened above my fear
I kept it until I could hear
And I'm so glad he's near
I remembered every tear
But the good about my manhood
Is that it's always been for good
On that foundation I've always stood
But they didn't do that in Hollywood
The way they did I didn't know he would be back
There are things you can't overcome if you're black
That was a near fatal attack
But since he's back on track
With cameras following him everywhere
I want him to know that I'm still here
Still a supporter on the front line in my seventh year
And so I said damn yeah
I'm proud to be a knight
I've carried on the fight
I've been through the darkest night
I've stood up for what was right
Alone I've watched the torch burn
Waiting for him to return
The kingdom was nearly ruined
It had lost its magic wand
There was no comfort from the cold
No blanket for my soul
And I'm getting too old
But through it all I did not fold

IX

Under incredible freight
He's tried to stand up straight
He held up that heavy weight
And the show will start at eight

I see new people on the scene
And I know he's only a human being
As I think about the bad things I've seen
Long time supporters fleeing
Knights leaving the round table
I didn't think I would be able
I didn't think I would be stable
Until I saw him on cable
And once again I know
I was right even though
It wasn't a game for me — so
I tried to be a stand up Negro
I had to stand for what he gave
I couldn't be a mindless slave
There was a world to save
Roads to justice to pave
His case stayed on my mind
It was something I had to rhyme
And I thought so in every line
I did so time after time
His perfection in every show
Kept my mind tight and on the go
I stayed on my post oh I know
It was more than 7 years or so
And when I left it was time to go
I didn't make much dough
I had responsibilities and although
For him there was a lot of woe
Because the Press wouldn't let go
There was nothing I could do but oh
I never closed that window
I never played Nintendo
I never changed my interest
I withstood every test
But I knew he was the best
Rock and roller in the west
So I'm not sorry at all

As a knight I answered the call
The kingdom did not fall
And he is still on sale in the mall

X

It's been months since the twins fell
Al Qaeda has caught hell
The Taliban has fallen as well
You don't shoot at the Liberty Bell
And not catch hell
And well-well-well
Is this coffin for sale?
I want Bin to look well on his way to hell
He made a lot of noise
He hit the big boys
And he did rejoice
But freedom of choice
Has been an American decree
Which says don't fuck with me
I afraid that line he didn't see
All he saw was his Jihad fantasy
And he didn't read
And so they bleed
And so yes indeed
I was glad but now back to Michael's lead
I thought he looked good with his brothers
They are such music lovers
They will look good on the new CD covers
They are a bunch of handsome brothers
When I woke up today
Again I thought no one is like MJ
Even though his brothers still play
The crowd came to see MJ
I mean he's got it that way
And he is still all they say

That's why we love MJ
But still social decay
Has changed our world a lot
We're lining up another shot
Because Al Qaeda has made us hot
We want to give them all we got
And blessed be Allah's name
And Bin it's really a shame
But Heaven isn't the blame
In Hell go make your claim
There you can feel the pain
That you caused with these insane
Acts of violence that were awfully inhumane
There you can be the son of Cain

XI

My hope is to go to Neverland
See Michael and hear his band
For me it will be like visiting the Promised Land
I know he's in sold out demand
I'm not gon' overstress being black
I'm really glad to see him back
When he dances I still react
That part of me is still intact
His new CD is called Invincible
And for me it's indispensable
I've heard parts of it on cable
I'm gon' get it when I'm able
You know fans are talking about it
They won't live without it
Wal-Mart is on my route
I got to get there before they sell out
I want to exit this on a happy note
We have seen enough cutthroat
Activity to make us feel remote

Whatever it takes the President has my vote
We can't turn back the clock
And after the nine eleven shock
I really feel like setting on the dock
But you got to move forward in Rock
I remember dancing to Billie Jean
Back then things weren't so mean
Michael really ruled that scene
There was hope in his routine
He made me look inside
Across those rivers of pride
He was my mystic guide
I saw sunsets on the evening tide
I planted flowers throughout my mind
I saw things to which I had been blind
And because he was so kind
There were always good things to find
Every evening I rushed home
And I put his records on
I didn't answer my phone
I was in my Michael Zone
I tried to dance although not like him
I have never been that smooth or trim
He was then and still is a gem
And I wanted to sing and dance like him

XII

We love you Michael came from the crowd
They were on their feet and they were loud
Besides feeling great joy I was very proud
Suddenly the mist became a dissipating cloud
His brothers left and there was just him
Still looking witty, smart, and trim
He was still an absolute rock and roll gem
And he had that R and B soul in him

He broke out with a favorite: "Billie Jean"
And from all over there came a great scream
It was like being in some kind of dream
He did the moonwalk and the moonwalk was mean
Again we love you Michael came from the crowd
He had emerged into the lights from a dark cloud
He was on the stage and the music was loud
He was slipping and moving and so well endowed
With artistry no one in the world could touch him
I was so glad that I had written about him
Obviously once again the world would select him
To wear again the crown of pop for them
I had only heard two songs from "Invincible" out
But I understood what the crowd was screaming about
The people in that audience had no doubt
They knew he could turn it out
If darkness came it wasn't coming that day
Nothing could've dimmed the light around MJ
He was a hit and he hit a long way
For me he brought back yesterday
I felt younger as I danced in my den
I was with him and I knew we were free men
The concert looked and sounded like Heaven
But by the time it aired it was after September eleven
But I don't want to feel that evil now
I was watching Michael and I knew somehow
His peace could be felt in Peking and Moscow
He was so majestic when he did his bow
Oh, real king or not, what does it matter?
He was my knight and he was back from a great battle
Though in New York people were slaughtered like cattle
The planes hit and dust and glass and blood did scatter
But this night we love you Michael came from the crowd
The place was jumping and the music was loud
Elizabeth was there and I could see Michael felt so proud
To be loved by so many as he dazzled the crowd

Chorus

Thank you God: you have done so much
To give us back his musical touch
Without it in our heart, our search
Through the darkness becomes too much
But he is back and we are so glad
In his presence the world seems less mad
His goodness has done so much
To eradicate evil Lord we need his touch
So I thank you God I thank you God
So I thank you God for giving us Michael back
And we feel the same whether white or black
So I thank you God I thank you God

The End

Afterthought

I would like to thank you if you have taken this journey with me. Michael remains a legend and I feel fortunate to have witnessed his time on earth. What was conceived in writing this has produced a time of spiritual growth for me; I strongly feel that rap will become a part of our spirituality. It already has a preaching delivery style and it is message oriented. I can see nothing but growth for the process. In my own way, I have tried to extend that vision. I have five other books in this style; please look for them in the not too distant future. Again thanks for taking this trip. I thank you for me and I thank you for Michael.